Rethinking self-sabotage

How to work with, not against, yourself to unlock your full potential.

NADINE EKIYA ABENG

ISBN 978-1-0687056-0-1

NEA

Dedication

For my beautiful 'Go Girls' Olivia, Amalia and Seraphina. You came through me to bring your glorious light to the world.

Thank you for choosing me as your guide. I am so grateful that I get to be your mum.

As you grow in mind, body and spirit, always know you are enough.

I Love you.

Special Thanks

I am grateful to each and every soul whose life has touched mine, for it is in those transactions that the seeds of my experience were sown.

I am grateful to the adults who nurtured me and to those who chastised me—I needed you all. Thank you.

I thank my children and my husband for their unending patience. I love the life we have; thank you for co-creating it with me.

I am grateful to the clients whose lives prompted me to pen this book. Together, we are bringing light and love to the world. Thank you.

Finally, to my mum, who walked this path before me, I am forever and deeply grateful for the signs. I carry your memory with me every day. I love you.

Table of Contents

Foreword 7

Introduction...13

Chapter 1: You Are Enough: The World Needs You and the Gifts You Bring........120

Chapter 2: Self-Sabotage: What It Is and Why We Do IT.......................................29

Chapter 3: The Power of Beliefs............45

Chapter 4: Authenticity, Acceptance, and the Highest Order..................................60

Chapter 5: Getting Out of Your Way......72

Chapter 6: Mindfulness.........................94

Chapter 7: Inner Child Work...............117

Chapter 8: Shadow Work....................146

Chapter 9: Creating a Compelling future 175

Conclusion..194

References..200

Using this book:

At the end of each section I have included a blank page for your reflections or brief notes.
However, I do recommend that you get a good journal so that all your exercises and reflections are in the same place.
The exercises and activities are intended to get you started and are a guide only. When you have done them a few times, feel free to adapt or amend them in line with your intuition – your soul knows what you need to do!

Ok, let's get started...

Foreword

Honestly, most people looking at my life wouldn't expect that I'd have anything to complain about. But, let's be honest – nobody can know the achings of your heart if you hide them well enough. And that's what I had become very good at doing – hiding my truth, and my pain. That realisation was, for me, my first sign that I was self-sabotaging.

I knew, deep down, that I wanted my life to be different, to feel different. But there was no way I was letting anyone else know that. Not even those closest to me were allowed to see my shortcomings or my deepest desires.

Deep down, though, I knew that if I didn't acknowledge my pain, at least to myself, I would not be able to move past it.

I had been doing all the 'outside' things – listening to inspirational people (and secretly disbelieving them!), reading books, and consuming podcasts.

I knew, in theory, what I needed to be doing to change my life. But try as I might, I couldn't get the habits to stick. There were always legitimate other things I needed to be doing instead of working on myself. That, in itself, is a form of self-sabotage – avoidance. I was always too busy with the demands of my life – mother of 3 children, all under 4 years old at the time, husband, family, friends, and full-time career as a primary school teacher – I had no time for myself, let alone self-improvement!

I spent years existing in my 'organised' mess before I eventually realised that even my busyness was another example of my own self-sabotaging – who knew?!

After a particularly challenging altercation at work one day, having uprooted my nuclear family to a new city more than 200 miles from the rest of my family and friends and still not finding fulfilment with the new job, bigger house, and slower pace of life, I collapsed in a heap and just sobbed. My husband, shocked to his core as he'd literally never seen me cry, didn't know what to do.

Hours later, a glaring realisation hit me – this was all my fault. I was the only consistent factor in the series of miserable events I was calling my life.

I stopped crying and turned my attention to

what I could do next, in the pursuit of fulfilment and happiness. While my job brought its challenges, I knew that it was not the root of the problem and was not to blame for my unhappiness.

I knew that leaving the job that provided the main income source for our family was not going to help. That said, I wanted desperately to be released from the demands of educational leadership and to be free to follow an even more passion-led career.

Though my job needed addressing I couldn't just up and leave. I decided to re-train as a life coach, and it was in the process of training and then working with other women that I began learning about myself and finally started making progress with my own life.

Today, though much improved, I must admit I am far from finished with my transformation.

There is still much I'd like to do to consolidate my personal improvement. But I felt compelled to record and share my journey so far.

There is so much content out there from 'finished products', and honestly, whenever I'd read or listen to them, I'd feel a weird combination of inspiration, resentment, and disbelief. Their words were inspiring, to be sure. But I'd feel resentment that they had been able to find traction with their actions where I had not. Why them and not me? It's not fair, I'd inwardly lament!

Then too, the disbelief – they've made that story up as part of their 'money-making' venture to sell their book or self-help course and so on.

So here it is. My in-progress reflections about my self-improvement journey and my ongoing relationship with self-sabotage. I'll cover my experiences with:

- Recognising common triggers (both events and people)
- Learning that I am enough
- Living in the now
- Embracing patience
- Focusing on progress, not results
- Getting out of my own way – noticing my patterns
- Exploring motivation and finding what works for me
- Working with my emotions and not against

them

- Understanding my thought patterns
- Bringing greater awareness to my life experiences

I wish I could say – do what I've done; it will work for you, but I can't. All I can say is this is what I've experienced, and this is what has worked for me so far.

There is every chance that I'll pen another book when I actually am that finished product that I am currently striving for, and that book may well contradict everything I've written here.... that is a risk I'm happy to take.

All I know is where I am right now, in the spring and early summer of 2024.

My hope for you is that you find companionship with me in this book. I am walking this path of constant learning and renewal with you. You are not alone – I am transforming, too, so if you have experiences or wisdom to share, please reach out to me!

Four reasons we change

We change when:

1. we've been hurt enough we have to.

2. we've seen enough we're inspired to.

3. we've learned enough that we want to.

4. we've received enough that we are able to.

Dr John C Maxwell

Introduction

** Sarah **

I had arrived at my job interview full of excitement and a sense that I would impress the interviewer and nail it. That job would be mine! My confidence gave way to self-doubt when the interviewer started to tell me about the position. Even though I met the qualifications, I started wondering if I would be able to handle the position, and I thought that maybe I was fooling myself for even attempting to obtain this position.

By the end of the interview, I felt defeated. All I wanted to do was to go back home and continue working at my current position, a position that I did not enjoy, but at least it was in my comfort zone.

** Jane **

Having recently listened to a book by Louise Hay and learned about the importance of protecting the information that my subconscious was exposed to,

I'd committed to not engaging in gossip with my friends and colleagues.

'How hard can it be?' I'd thought to myself, somewhat naïvely, I now realise. I'd gotten through the weekend just fine, meeting new people and exploring the Mind, body, and spirit show that had come to my city. It was wonderful to connect with so many spiritually minded people, and I felt re-energised when Monday morning came.

In the office, recounting weekend escapades and listening to the activities of others felt uplifting. But then, an email popped up – an unscheduled meeting had been scheduled. And, of course, the speculation began amongst the team, including the supposed 'backstory' for what might have happened, why and to whom.

A group of colleagues were talking in hushed whispers, and though I had been determined to keep my conversations 'clean', there was a part of me that was just itching to know what was going on. So, I went over and joined in. That familiar feeling in the pit of my stomach welcomed me, and the corners of my mouth twitched in anticipation of the news I was set to hear.

The week continued in that vein when an article popped up on my social feed with an update on celebrity shenanigans... Why is it so hard – everyone gossips; it can't be that bad, I reasoned to myself. And with that, my good intentions were dashed. Listening to the next part of the book completely slipped my mind, and it was months before I picked up the thread again.

** *Aziza* **

Finally, my business was beginning to generate interest (and income). After several smaller contracts and one-off bookings, a chance conversation at a conference led to my negotiating the biggest contract I'd had so far.

I was proud of the reputation I was building and excited to deliver the actual work. I set about preparing and had done all the research and planning needed to deliver the sessions. I'd organised childcare, and I'd even declined a social event, thinking that I'd want a good night's sleep ahead of this event.

But I didn't sleep – I ended up staying up late, scrolling my social feed and then watching a fascinating documentary on my favourite streaming platform. I was prepared, so I reasoned that I was ready.

Predictably, I woke up feeling less than refreshed and with little time for my morning routine. I was irritable and snappy with my children, whom I'd also woke later than was ideal. We were all rushing, and ultimately, I ended up late for the event.

My solid reputation earned me the good graces of the contractor and the delegates, who were more understanding than I thought I deserved. The day went well, and though I felt everyone was happy, it didn't turn into any repeat business, and I knew that I'd unwittingly damaged my reputation.

****

Has anything like the events in these scenarios happened to you? Have you ever found yourself striving to achieve something only to do something that ruined your chances for success?

What I have just described are examples of self-sabotage. When we self-sabotage, we stand in our way, unintentionally slowing our journey toward achieving our goals.

Every time we self-sabotage, we further damage our self-esteem. Our self-confidence takes a hit, and we retreat to the familiarity of our comfort zone. From this, a vicious cycle is created, as every failed attempt proves to us that we are not good enough to succeed. Fear not, however, because you can transcend this behaviour and bring yourself into a position for elevated success.

Traditional beliefs around self-sabotage seem to hold that there is a part of our Self 'acting out' and that we need to engage in battle to tame, control, harness or otherwise overcome that part.

In truth, setting out to 'fight' any part of your Self actually creates internal conflict and cultivates the very inharmony that you are seeking to move past.

Fighting is not the way. It is this philosophy that drove me to write this book. What I know in my heart and from my experience with my coaching clients is that we need self-compassion to move beyond self-sabotaging behaviours.

We need to learn to appreciate every aspect of our Self, including those aspects that are causing us to self-sabotage in the first place.

The subconscious mind always has a positive intention it is playing out. Even when the result of that intention is problematic, the intention itself is always positive.

I invite you to join me as we explore a more spiritual approach to healing. In this approach, we'll honour every part of ourselves and bring about healing through self-acceptance.

Notes

The universe does not make mistakes.

You (and your nuances) are deliberate.

Chapter 1

You Are Enough:

The world needs you and the gifts you bring

Who are you, and how did you come to be? More importantly, where did you get the idea that you are in any way comparable to others? If you were supposed to be comparable, you would have been made that way. Your consciousness is like no other, and none is like yours. You are you, wonderful you. Make of yourself what you will, but do it with the full understanding of your glory.

The universe does not make mistakes. The universe creates; it does not replicate. Therefore, everything and every person that exists is unique – nothing compares to you! Given that the universe does not make mistakes, you (and your nuances) are deliberate.

Furthermore, they are necessary for the flow of life on our planet. You are needed. Without you, there is some other aspect of life on the planet that is unable to operate in the way that is required.

For there to be relaxation, there must first be unrest. For there to be forgiveness, there must have been something that needed to be forgiven. So, let's lay to rest the notion that you are not enough – you are everything you need to be to serve this moment you are in. If, in a future moment, you need to be more, you automatically will be.

Now, let's take a moment to consider what a miracle your life actually is. Your body is made up of trillions of cells, each specifically designed to serve a special function. The muscles of our body can function because the muscle cells are doing their job. Muscle cells have a special structure that makes movement possible when working together.

The same is true with nerve cells and the cells in our blood. Nerve cells get the job done by aiding in the transmission of nerve impulses so that the body can function. Blood cells use their potential to carry oxygen to the different parts of the body. Each of these cells expresses its full potential by functioning according to its purpose.

This natural expression of potential is found throughout the natural world. An eagle soars majestically across the sky as it uses its powerful vision to detect prey, which can be miles away. The sapling of a redwood tree can reach towering heights as an adult, and like the eagle, it does so effortlessly.

There is a natural intelligence that orchestrates everything in the universe. Be it a single cell, an eagle, or a sapling, all these things carry out their natural potential effortlessly.

As humans, we, too, are part of this natural intelligence. However, unlike the rest of the natural world, our potential is unlimited. A nerve cell cannot do the job of a muscle cell. An eagle cannot dive underwater like a pelican, and a redwood sapling cannot grow up to be a cactus.

What makes humans unique is that we have unlimited potential for expressing who we are. A racist can become an anti-racist, advocating for civil rights, and a homeless person can become a millionaire.

These examples are based on the true stories of

Claiborne Paul Ellis and Chris Gardner, though there are many other examples to draw on. Each of these individuals evolved beyond their circumstances and expressed their natural potential for greatness. It did not happen right away, obviously, but it did happen.

Each of these individuals had to go through a personal journey before they were able to express their greater potential. In recognising their natural potential, these individuals did their jobs to become more fully actualised and to carry out their purpose. They came into the world and were able to develop their potential so that they could spread their gifts by making a positive impact on the lives of others.

Who you are at this moment is just the way you were intended to be. Since your birth, you have had your own unique experiences of the world. It is the culmination of those experiences that made you who you are today. Yet your potential is unlimited, even though it may not seem that way to you right now.

The only reason you do not recognise your

greatest potential is that you have allowed your lived experience of life, your past, to shape your potential rather than allow your potential to shape your experiences. All of us are this way; we allow our perceptions of life to define us. When those perceptions are limited, we experience ourselves the same way - limited.

Regardless of who you are or what your story is, know that the truth of who you are has yet to unveil itself. As with your potential, the truth of who you are is unlimited. What defines you at any moment in life is your beliefs about yourself. Now, it is time to let your potential shape your beliefs about who you are. It is time to begin an inner journey where you start expressing your greater potential so that you can offer more of your gifts to the world.

Notes

Notes

Self-sabotage can only exist in a fearful mindset.

It comes from the soul and personality being misaligned.

Gary Zukav

Chapter 2
Self-Sabotage:
What It Is and Why We Do IT

Self-sabotage can be described as behaviours that go against your conscious intentions. For example, let's say that you have set the goal of losing weight. Although at the conscious level, you want to achieve your goal, you continue to buy doughnuts and crisps for your cupboards. You tell yourself that you have the determination to eat them sparingly, yet you find yourself overindulging on them whenever you feel stressed. This is an example where you are consciously aware that you are self-sabotaging, but you do it anyway.

Sometimes, however, we self-sabotage without being aware of it. An example of this is when you go for a job interview for a position that you really want. During the interview, it is mentioned that the job involves travel, and you are asked how you feel about that. You respond by telling the interviewer the things you would need to do to make travel possible.

You were excited about the position and were aware of the job expectations before going for the interview. However, something happened during the interview that triggered something in your mind. Because of your response, you left doubt in the interviewer's mind that you would be the best candidate. You did not set out to do this consciously. Instead, you responded to your subconscious thoughts.

Theories on Why We Self-Sabotage

We all have our reasons for engaging in self-sabotaging behaviour, whether we are aware of the reasons or not. However, there are general theories to explain them:

Self-Worth

According to this theory, we believe, whether we are conscious of it or not, that we are not good enough or worthy enough to have those things in our lives that we desire. We may also believe that we do not deserve anything that we feel we did not earn. So, when the universe fulfils a desire of ours, we feel that there must be a mistake, that it was not meant for us.

The Past

If we experience the loss of something we desire, we may expect the same thing to happen in the future. To avoid repeating the pain of the past, we may self-sabotage to speed up the inevitable so that we can get the inevitable over with. An example of this is self-sabotaging a relationship because you expect it to end anyway.

A Need for Control

This theory states that we commit self-sabotage to gain a sense of control over our lives. Based on this distorted way of thinking, we gain a sense of control by holding ourselves responsible when things do not work out the way we want. We may still feel disappointed that things did not work out, but we can at least point to the reason, which gives us some sense of control in our lives.

The Soul and Personality

This theory enters the spiritual realm and was proposed by Gary Zukav (Lotus Pathway, 2018). To understand this theory, it is useful first to define the meaning of the soul and personality. The soul can be thought of as your higher self. It is eternal and without limits. It is the soul that makes you aware of your existence.

The personality is how the soul expresses itself and interacts with this world. Your lifetime experiences, including the familial and societal expectations of the time, shaped your personality.

All our experiences ultimately boil down to two forces: love and fear. We experience love when our souls and personalities are in alignment. When we experience love, we are aware of the oneness of life, that everything is interconnected, and that any sense of separation is just an illusion.

As a result, there is a knowing that nothing you desire is separate from you, including happiness and prosperity. Further, there is an understanding that every challenge we face has a sacred purpose; it is to help us connect with a deeper aspect of ourselves, which is the soul.

When our souls and personalities are not aligned, we experience fear. Because the connection with the soul is lost, the personality loses its sense of boundlessness and abundance. Instead, it behaves from a position of fear. A scarcity mindset develops, and we believe that we need to fight for everything that we want. Additionally, we suffer when we perceive that we have lost it.

Self-sabotage can only exist in a fearful mindset. It comes from the soul and personality being misaligned. When we are in a fearful mindset, we forget our true nature, which is an eternal being, and that we are the soul experiencing itself. We forget that we and the universe are inseparable from each other.

An example of this misalignment is a person who sabotages their relationships. The reason for their sabotage is they do not feel that they deserve to be in a loving relationship. What is required for this person to change their situation is for them to identify the erroneous belief behind their behaviour and to heal it.

Healing occurs when a person becomes aware of

the deeper aspects of themselves. This can be accomplished by seeking the help of a friend, coach or therapist who will be honest with them about their thinking and behaviour. It is from there that healing can begin. When the person develops the recognition of their essential being, they will no longer self-sabotage.

Women and Self-Sabotage

We women have the potential to do great things. The challenge is that we have been socialised through our culture to believe otherwise. Though this attitude is changing, there are plenty of women who hold on to this limiting view of themselves. Author Helene Lerner (Goudreau, 2012) has identified the nine most common ways that women self-sabotage themselves in the workplace:

Small Thinking

Despite their talents and potential, many women do not allow themselves to dream big. Lerner encourages women to seek a sense of purpose and live up to their potential.

Worrying

If you are feeling worried, overwhelmed, or scared about achieving your goals, Learner tells women to get used to these feelings. The point Lerner is making is that with all growth comes feelings of discomfort. She says the problem with many women is that they get caught up in the feelings of discomfort and focus on their worrying. Doing this is unproductive, and it drains all your energy. Plan for what may go wrong, but do not spend your time worrying about it.

Not Accepting the Total, You

It is important that you accept and honour all of you without exception. Honour your strengths and your perceived weaknesses. Appreciate all that you have accomplished while acknowledging your weaknesses. See your weaknesses not as a negative but as areas where you can grow. When you receive a compliment, accept it! When you are unsure of something, reach out for feedback from those who you trust. This is especially true in the workplace when you receive feedback that you are falling short in a certain area. After evaluating feedback, take action to improve the situation.

Not Being Authentic

Too often, women will not speak authentically. They may agree to something when they really are against it. They may not honestly express what they are thinking or feeling, which may be based on their past achievements, thus selling themselves short. When women learn to express how they feel, their opinions are more valuable, especially in the workplace.

Not Being Assertive

Lerner encourages women to become more assertive in the workplace so that more women can reach leadership positions. When you have the knowledge or skills regarding a work-related situation, dare to step up and do what you can to improve it. When women do not do that, they keep their potential hidden, which causes both them and the organisation to suffer.

Not Taking Time for Yourself

Many women are juggling multiple roles, including wife, mother, friend, and employee. Because of this, they do not take time for themselves. The problem is that you cannot be your best for others unless you are at your best. It is important that you take time for yourself to sit and reflect on your life and what matters most to you. It is also important to take time to have fun or to go on a holiday.

Keeping It to Yourself

Many women have trouble expressing their wants and needs, choosing instead to keep them to themselves. When doing this, we feel stuck in our lives. Acknowledge your wants and needs and move forward to fulfil them without feeling guilty about it.

Going It Alone

Just as with an organisation, we need our own board of directors in our lives. It is recommended that you build a team of personal and professional advisors to whom you can turn for feedback and support.

Not Empowering Other Women

Learner believes that women are not doing enough to pay it forward. As women move up in seniority, they need to help other women do the same. She believes that many women have the attitude that since they worked so hard to become successful, they want it all for themselves. The more women help others succeed, the more women there will be at upper levels of management.

Do You Find Yourself Doing Any of These Things?

So far in this chapter, I have given examples of self-sabotage. However, the way we self-sabotage can be quite varied. Here are some additional but common ways we self-sabotage:

Procrastination

Procrastination is one of the most common

forms of self-sabotage. We procrastinate because, at some level of our being, we perceive that doing the task will be more painful than not doing it. The pain of doing the task can come from the perception that trying to do the task will lead to failure or the disappointment of others. Curiously, it can also be due to the fear of succeeding. Some may fear that if they succeed in accomplishing the task, others will place more expectations on them.

Perfectionism

Perfectionism is not that dissimilar to procrastination. As with procrastination, there is a fear of failure. However, with perfectionism, the fear is that one's results will not be perfect. Perfectionists set unrealistic standards for themselves, which guarantees frustration or failure in achieving one's goal. With perfectionists, if anything goes wrong in achieving the task, they will feel like they failed.

Self-Medicating

Those who find themselves caught in a battle

between the desire to be successful and the belief that they are not good enough may seek comfort by self-medicating themselves using food, alcohol, drugs, or self-harm.

The following are some behaviour-specific signs that you may be self-sabotaging:

- You are often unprepared. An example of this is that you forget deadlines or do not properly prepare for important projects.
- You start projects, but you never see them to completion. Or you aspire to achieve things but never pursue them.
- You start a project that you are excited about, and things are going well. Yet, you come to a halt for no rational reason.
- You tell yourself things like:
  - "You could never achieve that."
  - "You don't deserve to have that in your life."
  - "If you try doing that, you will probably fail."

All of us have experienced these thoughts and behaviours at some point in our lives. For some of us, however, these thoughts and behaviours have become a pattern that we run repeatedly.

If this describes you, do not feel ashamed or feel like you are less. Instead, embrace it! I say this because if you do not acknowledge that you are self-sabotaging, then the behaviour will reinforce the limiting beliefs that you have about yourself, such as that you are not good enough. By acknowledging self-sabotaging behaviour, you can do something about it and you can change your life.

Chapter Exercise:
Time to Get Honest with Yourself

Now is the time to do some honest self-reflection to see if you are engaging in self-sabotaging behaviours. As mentioned, not all our self-sabotaging is done consciously. You can begin your self-discovery by asking yourself the following questions:

- Are your actions consistent with the goals that you are trying to achieve?
    - If your actions are not aligned with your goals, what is keeping you from changing your actions so that they are aligned?

- Are your actions consistent with your values?
    - If not, what is preventing you from taking action that is aligned with your values?
- Do you feel uncomfortable when you are making progress toward achieving your goals?
    - If your answer is “yes,” which of the following feels true to you:
        - Your feelings of discomfort are based on what others might think of you.
        - Your feelings of discomfort are based on your fear of failing or of looking foolish.
        - Your feelings of discomfort are based on the fear of success.
        - Your feeling of discomfort comes from the fear that you may achieve more than you planned.
    - If you do fear achieving more than you planned, is it because you believe that you will have more success than you deserve?

Based on what you have read in this chapter, decide whether you could be self-sabotaging. If you believe you are, why do you think you could be doing it?

Notes

The attention that we give our thoughts magnetises them.

One thought attracts another thought that is of the same quality or nature.

Chapter 3
The Power of Beliefs

In the last chapter, we learned about the basics of self-sabotage. The chapter discussed what self-sabotage is, theories on why we do it, and some of the ways we demonstrate this behaviour.

In this chapter, we are going to take a deeper look into why we do the things that we do, be it self-sabotaging or any other behaviour. If you have ever wondered why you make the decisions that you do, the answer to those questions boils down to your beliefs. It would not be an understatement to say that our beliefs are among the most powerful forces in the universe. Consider the following:

Our beliefs determine:

- What we focus on.
- What we overlook.
- What we are willing to do.
- What we avoid.
- How we see ourselves and how we see others.

We will begin this chapter with the most essential question: understanding what beliefs are.

What is a Belief?

Before we discuss how beliefs affect our lives, it is helpful first to understand what a belief is. But before we can do that, we first have to understand the nature of our thoughts. To begin this discussion, please do this simple exercise:

1. Take a moment to relax and close your eyes. To help you relax, take several deep breaths.
2. For the next minute or two, notice the thoughts that appear in your awareness. When doing this, it is important that you do not judge any thought that you experience. Have complete acceptance of any thoughts that arise.
3. Also, do not get involved with your thoughts. Don't get caught up in them or try to analyse them. Just be aware of them.
4. You can now your eyes.

Now let's consider some questions:

- Are you able to determine where your thoughts come from? Where were they before they appeared in your awareness? Where did your thoughts go when they left your awareness?
- Do you know what your thoughts are made of?
- Your thoughts were intangible; that is, they lacked colour, shape, or size, yet you knew of their presence. How were you able to do that?

If you were unable to answer these questions, do not be disappointed - no one can, even the greatest of scientific minds! The only thing that we know about thoughts is that they exist! Even though we know nothing about the nature of our thoughts, they obviously have a major impact on our lives, and that is putting it lightly.

It is my personal belief that thoughts are a form of energy, an intelligent energy. There is an intelligent force that orchestrates everything in this universe. Think about it: there are trillions of cells in your body, and each cell works in harmony and coordination with all the other cells. All of this is happening without any of your involvement.

Other examples of this natural intelligence that I speak of are the orderly patterns of the changing of the seasons and the orbiting of the planets. Animals and plants are continuously adapting their bodies and behaviours to meet their needs in a changing environment.

I believe that the thoughts that we experience are the result of our tapping into this natural intelligence. It has been estimated that the average person has 60,000 thoughts a day. Most of these thoughts pass through our consciousness undetected due to their fleeting nature. The reason for their fleeting nature is that they do not receive our attention as we do not find them meaningful to us. However, other thoughts do receive our attention. When this occurs, our thoughts are transformed.

Think about a time that you were trying to do something creative or you were problem-solving. In the very beginning, you may not have had an idea of where to start, or you just had a vague idea.

You turned your attention to the task that you were trying to accomplish, and eventually, you had a thought of how to approach the situation. As you continued to focus, other thoughts came to you that provided additional ideas. These thoughts continued to accumulate; they built on each other. Eventually, you developed a clear idea of how to go about the accomplishment of the task.

The attention that we give our thoughts magnetises them. When this happens, the original thought attracts other thoughts that are of the same quality or nature. The following is an example of this:

You have the thought, "Something seems to be wrong with my car." Because you have given this original thought your attention, it attracts a similar thought:

"The feel of the drive seems different. It is not a smooth ride."

Because you have given this thought your attention, it attracts another thought:

"I wonder if the engine is going bad or if I need a new transmission."

This thought then attracts other thoughts, such as:

"How am I going to pay for the repairs? I cannot afford it now."

This leads to the thought:

"How am I going to get to work if my car dies?"

This leads to the thought:

"How am I going to support my family?"

What has just been described is how beliefs are formed. The beliefs that are formed from this example may be:

- "I am failing as a provider for my family."
- "I can't trust the car dealer from which I bought this car."
- "Finding an honest mechanic will be difficult."
- "Life is always working against me."

Beliefs are a form of thought which we believe to be true. We have a sense of certainty that they are reality. Because of this sense of certainty, we may not question our beliefs. Unlike our thoughts, which are normally fleeting, our beliefs take up residence in our minds and become the lens through which we experience the world and ourselves. To better understand this, let's say that you put on a pair of yellow-tinted sunglasses. Because of the glasses, everything that you see will appear to be yellow.

Our beliefs are like tinted sunglasses. If I believe that most people are only looking out for their self-interest, that will be how they experience others, even those who are caring individuals. On the other hand, if I believe most people are good and will do the right thing, that will be my experience of them. The beliefs that we hold determine what we pay attention to. In turn, what we focus on determines the actions that we are willing to take and what gets deleted from our awareness.

Has this ever happened to you? You misplaced an object, and you look around to find it. After some time searching, you give up the search and move on. It is then you realise that the lost object was in your view of sight all that time. You did not see it. You did not see it because, at the time of your search, you were listening to your mind as to where you should look.

The Bannister Effect

The story of Roger Bannister can illustrate another example of the power that our beliefs have over us. Bannister is the first person to break the record for the one-mile run. Before Bannister's achievement, no one had run a mile in less than four minutes.

An important reason for Bannister's success came down to his belief system. Most runners were professionally trained. Because of their experience, most trainers did not believe that the one-mile run could be done in less than four minutes. As a result, they coached with that expectation.

Bannister was different as he had never been professionally trained, so he did not have this limiting belief. After Bannister demonstrated that the record could be beaten, other runners began to beat the four-minute record. It became so common, in fact, that Bannister's record became the new standard.

Beliefs and the Pleasure-Pain Principle

At the fundamental level, all living beings move toward potential pleasure while moving away from sources of potential pain. This is the determining factor of all human behaviour. Everything we do is based on the belief that we will either experience pleasure or avoid pain because of it.

Sometimes, we are faced with a situation where, no matter what we choose to do, we will experience unwanted consequences. In cases like these, we will decide to do what we believe will be the least impactful to us. With this understanding, we can begin to understand why we self-sabotage.

Let us say that Loretta is experiencing a lot of stress over her living situation. She does not like her job, and she feels burdened with responsibilities. Loretta understands that if she could improve her finances, she could pursue her goals and achieve a more fulfilling life. However, her stress sometimes makes her feel like she just cannot take it anymore. To make herself feel better, Loretta goes on shopping sprees. The problem is that her spending keeps her from advancing toward her goals.

This self-sabotaging behaviour is the result of Loretta's belief system, which associates spending money with pleasure. You may be thinking to yourself, "But wait! Loretta's behaviour is moving her in the direction of pain, the failure to achieve her goals." You are correct on this, but some clarification is needed. Unless we examine our beliefs and make sense of them, we will respond to our feelings in the short term rather than focusing on the long-term consequences.

Even though Loretta knows rationally that her behaviour is counterproductive, at the emotional level, she will respond to what she is feeling in the immediate term. We give in to our sabotaging beliefs because we have associated them with immediate pleasure, allowing us to get a temporary reprieve from the negative feelings that we are experiencing.

Given this, we can see that our beliefs, even our negative ones, are serving a purpose, even though they may lead to self-defeating behaviour. When we fail to examine our beliefs, they will point us in the direction of what we perceive is best for us at that moment while neglecting the long-term consequences.

The Subconscious and the Shadow Self

The previous scenario of Loretta provided an example of how when we do not examine our beliefs, they cause us to go on autopilot. Loretta knew her spending was causing her problems, but spending money helped her forget about the stressors in her life. Since the emotional pain she felt was more real than her future dreams, she reverted to her spending habits. She used spending money to feel better because, at some point in her past, she learned to associate spending money with pleasure. By repeatedly engaging in this behaviour, it became a habit for her.

Sometimes, however, we lack any awareness of those beliefs that guide our behaviour. Sometimes, we have a belief about ourselves that is so painful that we suppress it subconsciously. Even though we may suppress a belief, it will still influence our lives, causing us confusion as to why we are behaving the way we do. Here is another scenario to illustrate this:

As a child, Brianna was very friendly and loving. She was also very trusting of others. This kind of behaviour made her parents uncomfortable, and they gave her negative feedback when she acted this way. At some point, Brianna learned to associate her parent's disapproval with her own self-worth. She learned to believe that she was not good enough the way she was.

Because of this, Brianna began to distance herself from that part of herself and adopted a new persona, one that was more aligned with her parents' expectations. She learned to believe that to be good enough, she had to be more distant and reserved. Brianna began to develop a new sense of identity.

When Brianna got older, she started having relationships with men. This is the part of the story where I need to explain something that is of great importance. Remember the previous comparison of beliefs to tinted sunglasses? Well, that is another important piece of information that you need to know. We project our beliefs onto other people, including our subconscious beliefs. Remember, Brianna learned to associate pain with how she used to be.

Further, since Brianna suppressed that part of her life, she had no memory of being that way. This dynamic affected her relationships. When Briana encountered men who were friendly and loving, it made her uncomfortable; their behaviour was a turnoff for her. The reason for this is she was unconsciously projecting the emotional pain that she associated with the suppressed aspect of herself onto the men who had the same qualities. Instead, Brianna found herself attracted to men who were more distant and less trusting. In other words, Brianna found herself attracted to men who matched her false persona. The problem is that these men did not treat her well.

Brianna kept repeating this pattern of behaviour, which left her confused. She kept pursuing the same kind of men, and she kept ending up hurt. In turn, Brianna doubted her desirability, and her self-esteem suffered. All of this happened because she had denied an authentic aspect of herself and attempted to project a disingenuous version of herself to herself and others.

Chapter Exercise

Make a list of your beliefs that you believe are limiting you from experiencing the life that you desire.

Notes

Dreams.

How do you know
you had a dream?

Who are 'you' who
hears the thoughts
and watches the
dreams?

Chapter 4
Authenticity, Acceptance, and the Highest Order

You and I are multidimensional beings, meaning that we are comprised of multiple dimensions that co-exist. These dimensions include the physical, mental, and spiritual:

The Physical Dimension: The physical dimension is what we are most familiar with, and it consists of the world of form, which includes the body. Though your body may appear sold, this is just an illusion. In truth, the body, as with everything else in this universe, is an expression of energy. This has been demonstrated by quantum physics.

Quantum physics has shown that nothing in this universe is truly solid, including the atom, which for many years was considered to be a solid structure. Because of the way our minds work, we perceive ourselves and the objects of the world as being solid. It is this sense of physicality that allows us to distinguish ourselves from others. I know that I am not you or the tree in my garden because of our separate forms.

The Mental Dimension: The mental dimension consists of our thoughts, emotions, and perceptions, which is the mind. The mind is also essentially comprised of energy and is formless. The mind is the source of infinite potentiality. What this means is that there is no limit to the kind of thoughts, emotions, and perceptions that we can experience. Perceptions refer to how we experience ourselves and the world around us.

The Spiritual Dimension: The spiritual dimension has nothing to do with religion or spiritual thinking; rather, it refers to consciousness. Consciousness is the essential aspect of who we are. How is it that you can be aware of a thought or feeling? How is it that you can be aware of a new idea? How is it that you can know whether you had a dream or not the previous night? You can substitute the word "consciousness" with the words "knowing" or "awareness." We are aware of ourselves, and we are aware of what we are experiencing. In fact, there can be no experience without the awareness of it.

Both the physical dimension and the mental dimension are found within the spiritual dimension. In fact, the physical dimension and mental dimension are its expressions. In our daily lives, however, most of us are only aware of the physical and mental dimensions. Most of us have not taken the time to understand and connect with the spiritual dimension, the most essential aspect of ourselves.

When the Ego Comes to Play

While the essence of who we are is consciousness, we identify with the mind and body, which is to say that who we are is the mind and body. From this sense of identification, the ego is formed. The ego's purpose is to keep us safe from harm. Because of this, the ego is based on fear. We allow the ego to govern us because we have lost our connection with the essence of who we are, which is consciousness.

When we allow ourselves to be ruled by the ego, we are on constant guard to protect the image that we have of ourselves. The following are some of the ways that this shows up in our lives:

- The fear of looking foolish.
- The fear that we are not good enough.
- The fear of not being accepted for who we are.
- The fear that we are not lovable.
- The need to judge ourselves and others.

The ego is ultimately the driver of self-sabotage. When we experience something that the ego finds too threatening, it will lead us to suppress the thoughts and emotions associated with it. Remember Brianna's scenario? Her ego found her parents' disapproval too threatening, so she suppressed her authentic nature, which was friendly, loving, and trusting. In place of that, Brianna came up with a new persona, one that was more distant.

Embracing All of You is Freedom and Power

As mentioned, the physical and mental domains are found within consciousness. This means that everything that exists is interconnected with everything else. The mind is connected to the body, thoughts are connected to emotions, and the energy from which these things arise also gives rise to all our experiences.

There is nothing in our experience that is inherently good or bad; it just is. Rather, our minds create the meaning of our experiences. Our minds make judgments about what is good and what is bad. Because of this, our minds suppress aspects of ourselves, be they thoughts, memories, or feelings, that we find too threatening.

The mind does not recognise the interconnectedness of all that exists. Instead, it leads us to acknowledge some aspects of ourselves and disapprove of others. Those aspects of ourselves that we disapprove of may become suppressed. When this happens, we can no longer be our authentic selves. Instead, we become fragmented.

We want to learn to fully accept ourselves as we are now, regardless of what others may think of us. When we learn to embrace all aspects of ourselves, including those that we perceive to be negative, true healing can come. When we do this, those aspects of ourselves that we disapprove of will naturally support us in our happiness. The result is that we move from being fragmented to becoming whole.

No aspect of yourself is negative or inadequate. Rather, it is our own judgments, our beliefs that aspects of ourselves are negative or inadequate, that cause our suffering. It is not the aspects themselves.

It is for all these reasons that it is important to give up resisting any aspect of yourself. There is a saying, "What you resist, persists." Remember, if you are resisting something, then you are giving it your attention. As mentioned, most of our thoughts are fleeting. The only reason why some thoughts become beliefs is because we give them our attention. If there is an aspect of you that you want to change, focus on what you do want rather than resisting any aspect of your being. When you do this, the things that you want will have a greater influence on your life.

Chapter Exercise

Make a list of your past accomplishments, both personally and professionally. When doing so, do not just rely on what you were acknowledged for. Also, include those things that you accomplished that others may not have known about.

Notes

Notes

Every aspect of you has the potential to express itself in a way that supports your happiness or works against it.

What determines its functioning is how you perceive yourself.

Chapter 5

Getting Out of Your Way

In the remaining chapters of this book, you will find different techniques for recognising, embracing and transcending self-sabotage. However, before we explore the various techniques, we are going to start with the basics of healing, which involves honouring yourself.

As mentioned, no aspect of who you are is inherently negative or inadequate. Every aspect of you has the potential to express itself in a way that supports your happiness or works against it. What determines its functioning is how you perceive yourself.

Let's say there is a woman who is carrying with her a sense of shame for something that happened in the past. She avoids feeling that shame by distracting herself by drinking alcohol. Also, she does not pursue her dreams as she believes that she is unworthy. She has done this because she interprets the feeling of shame as evidence that she is a bad, unworthy person.

However, this interpretation of how she feels is just that, an interpretation. Every emotion that we experience holds a positive intent for our happiness. It is a message from universal intelligence that is here to serve us. From a higher perspective, the emotion of shame is telling us that we did something that went against our better judgment and that we need to learn from it. This emotion is not a message that we are bad or inadequate; it is simply that something bad happened and we'd want to be more conscious in similar situations to make more informed decisions.

Similarly, the emotion of sadness informs us that we have experienced a loss. It could be the loss of a relationship, an image that one had of oneself, or an object. However, sadness serves us in our development. It allows us to develop a greater appreciation for what we have. It can teach us how to avoid similar losses in the future. Both messages provide us with an opportunity to develop ourselves further.

If we allow ourselves to get lost in anger, we can turn against ourselves or others. However, when seen from a higher perspective, anger can mobilise us to take positive action that will benefit our own and others' lives.

Whenever you experience a “negative emotion,” see it as a teacher. It is sending you a message that you need to make a change in what you are thinking or doing. Everything in this universe is intended to support life itself, the greater good, and us if we are willing to get curious and have faith that we are being guided by something greater.

No aspect of you is a mistake. Remember what was mentioned before: there is an infinite intelligence in this universe that orchestrates everything within it. Anything that we perceive to be a mistake or flaw is a function of our minds. In other words, there is nothing in life that has an inherent meaning. Rather, we create the meaning of our experiences. To transcend any sabotaging behaviour, you first need to acknowledge the miracle that is you!

Developing a New Mind Set

The reason why you think and behave the way you do is because of your mindset, which consists of your beliefs. Your beliefs are like a computer program. A computer program determines how your computer functions and the tasks that you can do. In the same way, your beliefs determine what you think, what you pay attention to, and the decisions that you make. In this and upcoming chapters, you will find a variety of methods for creating a change in the way that you think and feel.

Getting Started

Before we get into specific ways to work with your self-sabotaging behaviour, we will start with the basic steps that need to be addressed to be successful in doing so. Moving forward, all the techniques described will fit into one or more of the following categories:

Becoming Aware

To change anything about ourselves, we first need to be aware of what needs to be changed. This may seem obvious, but so many people lack a clear awareness of how their thoughts and emotions affect their behaviour. So, the first step is to become aware of how you are sabotaging yourself. You can do that by reflecting on the following:

- Do you have a pattern of setting goals that are important to you but never follow them through to completion?
- Are there issues in your life that you need to make decisions on, but you keep delaying the decision?
- Do you lack motivation to get things done, even the things that are important to you?
- Is there an area in your life where you frequently fall short of completing for no real reason?
- Are there behaviours that you consistently do or do not do that create upset for others?
- Are there certain tasks that cause frustration for you because you know that you could do

a better job with them, but you haven't?

By honestly answering these questions and using the information from earlier parts of this book, you should be able to determine if you are self-sabotaging. When you become aware of this, you can then address it.

As a side note, if you realise that you are self-sabotaging yourself, it is important not to develop the mindset that something is wrong with you and you need to fix it. The idea that you need to fix any aspect of yourself goes against the spirit of this book. We need to fix things when they are broken, but you are not broken. Rather, you have not accepted aspects of who you are, so these aspects have been suppressed. It is the suppression of these aspects, not the aspects themselves, that is causing you problems. For this reason, see the bringing of awareness to these areas of your life not as a fix but as sunshine that lights up the dark.

Identify the Emotional Component

There is an emotional component that underlies all our behaviours. As mentioned, the function of our beliefs is to move us toward perceived pleasure and away from perceived pain. If I am self-sabotaging, it's because I have the belief that accomplishing the task will be less pleasurable than if I do not accomplish it. Ultimately, it's the emotional aspects that are driving my behaviour.

Self-sabotaging behaviour arises from negative emotions associated with the task. These emotions may include feelings of worthlessness, anger, or anxiety.

An example of this is that you may have not intentionally completed a task that your partner was depending on you to do. Earlier, your partner may have given you a look that made you feel that they did not appreciate you. This emotion triggers you to engage in self-sabotaging behaviour, not doing what your partner asked. In truth, the look that your partner gave you may have had nothing to do with you. They may have had things on their mind.

It is for this reason that learning to manage your emotions or self-regulation is an important aspect of working with self-sabotaging behaviour.

Information on how to do this can be found throughout this book.

Identifying Your Beliefs

It is important to remember that our beliefs and emotions are inseparable from each other. They are like two sides of the same coin. Your thoughts affect your emotions, and your emotions affect your thoughts. When you have identified the emotion that you are experiencing, it is important to identify the belief that is associated with it.

In the previous section was the scenario of you being triggered emotionally by the way your partner looked at you. Let's say the emotion you felt when this happened was that of anger. So, you would ask yourself, "What would I have to believe to feel this way?" By asking this question, you can see if there is supporting evidence to validate this belief or if you are having irrational thoughts. If your partner seemed fine before the incident, then it may be reactive thinking. Naturally, you can also ask them about it.

You can also develop greater awareness of your

self-sabotaging behaviour by keeping a journal. Write down what you say to yourself when you engage in self-sabotaging behaviour. Include any of your thinking, even if it seems silly or unimportant. This method works best when you are engaging in sabotaging behaviour. This way, you will get the information while it is fresh in your mind. If writing down your thoughts at the time of the behaviour is impractical, try making a voice recording as soon as you are able. You could also use memory tricks, such as image clues, to help you recreate the situation in your mind later when you are able to write it all down. You'll be amazed at how much you are able to recall – each memory thought triggers another. Like attracts like, as mentioned before.

Make a Change

Our emotions, beliefs, and behaviours are like links in a chain. The change of one link will change the other two. When you have identified the emotions and thoughts that lead to self-sabotaging behaviour, you can change them by challenging them.

You challenge your thoughts and emotions not by denying them or trying to control them. Rather, it is done by accepting their existence and focusing on empowering alternatives. These alternatives can be changing your beliefs and taking the actions that support your success. You can start this process by asking yourself empowering questions, such as:

- What can I tell myself that will empower me to succeed?
- What are my options for achieving my goal?
- How can I break down this goal into smaller ones so that I can increase my chances of success?

Creating a Shift in Your Beliefs

Remember the section on the pleasure-pain principle? It states that our beliefs function to move us in the direction of perceived pleasure and away from perceived pain. If you do not believe that you can do something, it is because you have a belief that associates pain with trying to accomplish it. Maybe you are afraid of what others may think if you do not succeed or that others will judge you for wanting to attain that goal.

Also, if you believe that just staying as you are will prevent you from being judged by others or risking failure, then that may seem safe to you, which is less painful than the thought of going for it. On the other hand, the reason why you are reading this book is likely due to the belief that doing so will lead to a pleasurable outcome, such as gaining new information that can improve the quality of your life. In this chapter, you will learn how to use these twin forces of pain and pleasure to make them work for you rather than being controlled by them.

Our beliefs are our mind's way of evaluating the world. The belief that the world is a dangerous place is intended to keep us safe from the perils of life. The belief that the world is full of wonder invites us to embrace the world and seek out all the amazing experiences that it has to offer. As stated earlier, both beliefs are purely subjective. They are not formed by reality; they are the mind's interpretation of reality. Obviously, there are dangers in the world, as there is magic and wonder.

One's conditioning determines the belief that one adopts. Let us say I grew up in a family that has a cynical view of the world. I was raised to believe that people would take advantage of you whenever they had the opportunity. I was also taught that life was about the survival of the fittest. If I showed vulnerability, or if I did not dominate, I would become the prey of someone stronger. Being raised with this kind of mentality will lead to the belief that the world is dangerous. That belief would be reinforced because I would be focusing on how the world could pose a danger.

Now, let us say that I was raised by parents who taught me to be curious about the world. Each day, they encouraged me to learn something new. They exposed me to documentaries about the world's wonders, and they taught me to respect others. They shared their enthusiasm for life with me. This kind of conditioning will lead me to believe that the world is a place of wonder. This belief would be continuously reinforced because my focus would be on learning about this world and exploring its wonders.

Both beliefs serve their intended purpose. The first belief (the world is a dangerous place) helps keep me from the potential pain that the world could inflict on me. The second belief (the world is full of wonder) causes me to move toward the pleasures of experiencing the world's wonders.

However, both beliefs are one-dimensional. Because our beliefs determine what we focus on, there is a lot of information being overlooked. Having the belief that the world is a dangerous place means that everything good about the world is falling on the margins of my focus. Conversely, the belief that the world is wondrous means that I will not be as aware of the dangers that exist as someone who holds this belief. Whatever our beliefs are, they will continue to direct our lives if they remain unchallenged.

By creating a shift in our focus, we can get a more balanced view of our beliefs and determine how they benefit us and how they limit us. If I have the belief that the world is a dangerous place, a shift in my focus may reveal that the costs of holding this belief outweigh any benefits that I may be gaining.

If you are holding beliefs that prevent you from making your life the way you want it, all you need to do is create a shift in your beliefs. However, there is a challenge. You may be unhappy with your life and want to change it, but your limiting beliefs provide a comfort zone.

It is easy to dream of a better life but not do anything about it. New Year's resolutions are like this. We may make a resolution to lose weight but give up trying when we meet with frustration. Because we are wired to avoid pain, we revert to our old ways. It may not be what we want, but at least there is a level of comfort there.

To change your life, you first need to change your beliefs. To change your beliefs, you need to shift your focus. You need to focus on all the ways that your current beliefs are limiting you. When you have evaluated your beliefs, you need to shift your focus on all the benefits you would gain if you adopted a more empowering belief. The following are ways that you can do this:

Challenge Your Thinking

This simple method creates doubt in any limited thinking that you may have. The way it works is like a court trial, where decisions are based on the evidence. You challenge your thinking by looking for the facts. For example, someone may feel that they are not capable of becoming successful because of their past. They can challenge their thinking by asking themselves questions such as:

- "What evidence do I have that I cannot become successful?
- "What evidence do I have that my thinking is not correct?"

Other questions that you can ask yourself are:

- "What evidence do I have that contradicts my current thinking?"
- "This thing that I am worried about, how likely is it to happen?"
- "What would I tell a loved one if they were in my situation?"

The idea behind this questioning is to create doubt in your negative thinking so that you can make room for more empowering thoughts.

Belief Balance Sheet

This next exercise requires more work than the previous one, but it can also have a more powerful impact on your thinking.

You will need:

- Three sheets of paper
- A writing instrument

1. Think about something you would like to accomplish but find yourself holding back from doing it, such as leaving a bad relationship.
2. On the first sheet of paper, list all your thoughts about the task. When making your list, do the following:
    a) Write the first thing that comes to your mind.
    b) Write as fast as you can, and do not worry about neatness or grammar.

c) Keep writing until you run out of things to write.

3. When you have completed your list, choose the one that you believe is most responsible for your staying as you are. Example: "I believe leaving the relationship will just make things harder for me."
4. Take the second sheet of paper and fold it in half lengthwise.
5. On the top of the paper, write down the belief that you selected.
6. On the left-hand side of the paper, brainstorm how this belief has cost you in your life. Ask yourself how it has affected you emotionally, in your self-esteem, how it has affected your health, in your relationships, spiritually, and in your finances.
7. When writing, keep in mind the following:
   a) Write as fast as you can. Do not spend time thinking about it.
   b) Write down the first thing that comes to your mind, even if it seems irrelevant.

c) Feel the emotions that arise as you write. This is a heartfelt exercise, not a thinking one.

d) Keep writing until you run out of things to write.

8. For each item that you wrote down, assign an arbitrary point value as to how much impact this item has had on you. When selecting the point value, choose the first number that comes to mind.
9. When you have completed assigning the point values, add up all the point values and place the total at the bottom of the page.
10. For the right side of the page, repeat Steps 6-9 with one exception. Instead of writing down all the ways that this belief has cost you, write down all the ways that it has benefited you.
11. When you have completed step 10, compare the scores on each side – is the thought serving you?
12. Now, try to think of a new alternative belief that empowers you. Example:

Original belief: "I believe leaving the relationship will just make things harder for me."

New belief: "Leaving the relationship may be hard, but it will be worth it."

13. On the third sheet of paper, repeat steps 4-10 using your new belief, with the following exception: Reverse Steps 6 and 10. For Step 6, write down all the ways you believe you would benefit from adopting your new belief. When doing step 10, write down all the ways you believe your new belief would cost you.
14. When you have completed the two sheets, do the following:
    a) Immediately review your lists, allowing yourself to experience any emotions that arise fully.
    b) Review your lists every day, once in the morning and once before you go to bed for twenty-one days.

This chapter explored how our beliefs create our experience of the world and how our limiting beliefs prevent us from moving forward in life. However, even if we have empowering beliefs, we still need to focus our attention on creating the life we desire. Unless focused, our attention will be scattered, which is the topic of the next chapter.

Chapter Exercise

In your journal, write about what you learned from challenging your limited beliefs.

Notes

We don't meditate to get good at meditation.

We meditate to get good at life.

Chapter 6
Mindfulness

There is a story about a servant whose master was never seen by him. The master, who lived in a large castle, would never venture from his room. Every morning, the servant would go to his master's room to receive his instructions for the day. Because of his master's peculiar behaviour, the servant would receive his instructions on a message left outside of his master's door.

One day, the servant was talking to the maid about how frustrated he had become with his master. He explained to her how his master was never satisfied and that nothing was ever good enough for him. The maid suggested to the servant that he should talk to his master about it.

The servant decided to follow through with the maid's suggestion and went to the master's room to speak to him. When the servant arrived at the master's room, he noticed that the door was open! Never in all his years of service had the servant seen this before! Out of concern for his master, the servant entered the room to see if his master was in trouble. It was then that the servant's concern turned into disbelief; the room was empty! There were no furnishings, no rugs, and no master!

The servant realised that for all these years, he had been serving a master who did not exist.

This story of the servant and his master is a metaphor for our relationship with our minds. We are the servants, while the mind is the master. We have loyally followed the messages of the mind, which is why we often behave in ways that do not support us.

However, we can free ourselves from our loyalty to the mind and become its masters. The ancient practise of mindfulness provides us with the means to do this.

The Wisdom of the Ancients

We live in a time that is unprecedented in human history. Today's standard of living would be considered science fiction or fantasy fifty years ago. We have 24-hour media cycles, high-speed internet, quantum physics, GPS, driver-less cars and other technologies that offer us greater opportunities for enhancing our lives than ever before.

Despite all these advances, the level of our collective happiness, fulfilment, and wisdom has not kept pace. Despite all our advances, we have not invested the same kind of determination in understanding the nature of who we are. We have forgotten who we are at the most fundamental level of our being, and that amnesia is preventing our innate wisdom from shining through.

Our undisciplined mind is eclipsing this wisdom. We live out our lives with an endless parade of thoughts passing through our consciousness, many of which preoccupy our attention. The purpose of mindfulness is to transcend our thoughts, thus quieting the mind.

Think about your life. What is preventing you from experiencing inner peace? What prevents you from experiencing true happiness, happiness independent of other people, situations, or events? We may believe that happiness or inner peace is contingent upon getting some result in our lives.

We may be looking for a healed relationship or freedom from an existing relationship. We may also be looking to overcome our past or forgive ourselves. Perhaps we are looking to overcome financial hardship or physical illness.

Regardless of what we are looking for, it will not lead to true happiness. If we fail to achieve the results that we are looking for, we will either give up or continue to try.

If we achieve the result that we were looking for, we may enjoy the feeling of happiness and success, but it will only be temporary. Our sense of victory will diminish with time, and we will start the cycle anew. In this way, we are like hamsters on a wheel. No matter how much energy we put into our efforts, we often find ourselves back where we started.

To experience wholeness, happiness, and inner peace, one must learn to live in the present moment. Mindfulness makes this possible. When we are mindful, we can transcend the mind and recognise that our individual lives are inseparable from life itself.

To practise mindfulness is to awaken from the illusion of being separate from life and experience lasting happiness and well-being. More importantly, we can make a difference in the lives of others. If enough of us learn mindfulness, we can change the future of this planet.

Mindfulness is not a form of spiritual thought, nor does it involve adopting a belief system. In fact, practising mindfulness is inaccurate, as practising mindfulness implies that there is something to practise. Rather, mindfulness means taking the time to notice what exists already. If you persist in exploring mindfulness, you will experience your life in a whole new way.

What is Mindfulness

Trying to explain mindfulness is like trying to express the joys of eating chocolate mousse to someone who has never eaten it. In our busy, fast-paced society, with all its distractions, most of us spend a significant portion of our lives not living mindfully. We are unaware of life in the present moment because our minds are carrying us off to a different time and place. We get caught up in our thoughts of the past or the future, oblivious of the richness of the present moment.

Mindfulness is not just a spiritual or metaphysical practise that mystics or seekers engage in; it is both a vital aspect of our happiness and a precious gift that comes with being conscious. Without mindfulness, we cannot become fully actualised human beings; rather, we become reactive to situations and events. Instead of using our potential to expand our awareness, our lives are based on a stimulus-response existence.

To live mindfully is to be fully aware of what is happening now, at this moment. When we practise mindfulness, we become aware of everything happening within and around us. Our awareness is concentrated on what we are experiencing at the moment, and we experience the moment with complete openness and acceptance.

To be fully actualised as a human is to be able to access the wisdom and awareness that is needed to create value, a value that benefits both ourselves and others. This value creation can only come from being fully aware of what is happening at the present moment, both within and outside us. Without this awareness, we stumble through life and often create suffering for ourselves and others.

Why Being Mindful Matters

Our place in life is intimately connected to all of existence. If you were to pull a single strand of a spider's web, the entire web would experience your pull. Developing mindfulness enables us to respond to life in a manner that considers how our thoughts, feelings, emotions, and actions are directly linked to life's web. The quality of our lives is directly proportional to our level of awareness of it.

A lack of mindfulness is one of the biggest reasons for unhappiness. While engaged in thought, we cannot be fully aware of the emotions and feelings that lie within us. We all have emotions or feelings that we try to avoid experiencing. When we self-sabotage, we perpetuate our reactions to painful feelings that we experienced in the past.

Emotions and feelings are energy forms, and if not expressed, they may manifest in negative ways. Just as with thoughts, emotions within themselves are powerless. They are only as powerful as the amount of attention we give them or when we suppress them. To become mindful of your emotions, treat them as you would a guest. Allow them to come and go without trying to control them.

Because you acknowledge and accept your thoughts and emotions, your resistance toward them will dissolve. This brings about healing. You will no longer be fragmented; you will become whole. When this occurs, every thought and emotion will serve its highest purpose, which is to support your well-being.

Why Mindfulness Works

Before we discuss how and why mindfulness works, we need to discuss the nature of the mind. Imagine that you are in a theatre watching a movie. This movie is full of drama, suspense, action, and comedy. You lose awareness of everything that is happening around you; the movie totally absorbs you.

With each passing scene, you experience a shift in emotion. During the movie, you experience anticipation, concern, fear, anger, happiness, sadness, laughter, and suspense. Your state of being is as though it is on a roller coaster ride as each scene elicits a change in how you feel.

Now imagine this situation: you are watching the same movie and enjoying all the range of thoughts, feelings, and emotions that come from experiencing it; however, you are also fully aware of what is happening around you in the theatre. You are aware that it is just a movie, and do not get caught up in it. The movie may elicit a wide range of emotions from you, yet a sense of peace or calm remains with you. You enjoy your movie experience fully while never forgetting it is just a movie.

These two scenarios are a metaphor for life. You are the one watching the movie while the movie is in your mind. The first scenario represents the lives of most of us. We are absorbed in our thoughts, memories, beliefs, and perceptions. All of these contribute to shaping our sense of identity and life experience. Without exception, all our problems and sufferings, whether they are individual or collective, arise because we are absorbed in our minds; we are absorbed in the movie.

With mindful practise, we come to realise that we are not our thoughts, emotions, or other mental functions; rather, we are the witness of these mental functions as they arise within us. To demonstrate this, do this exercise:

1. Sit or lie down and close your eyes. Allow yourself to relax.
2. Enhance your relaxation by focusing on the flow of your breath. Breathing normally, focus on the flow of your breath as you inhale and the flow of your breath as it leaves your body during exhalation.
3. As you relax further, visualise a beautiful sunset in as much detail as possible.

Note: Everyone visualises, though this ability varies from person to person. Some people can see their visualisations in vivid detail, while the visualisations of others can be very vague or faint. This does not matter. Just make your visualisation as real as possible according to your ability.

4. Now, visualise a black cat and see it as vividly as possible.
5. Lastly, visualise a full moon. Again, make it as real as possible.
6. Now, open your eyes.

During this visualisation exercise, you visualised a beautiful sunset, a black cat, and a full moon. At no time did you confuse yourself with any of these visualisations. You knew that you were not the sunset, the black cat, or the full moon; you were the observer of these things. These visualisations were just thoughts that took on a visual dimension.

You did not identify with these thoughts. The reason for this is that your mind did not consider these thoughts to be important, so you did not identify with them. On the other hand, when you are triggered, you likely place great importance on certain thoughts.

With mindful practise, one becomes aware of the mind's activity without becoming reactive to it. This kind of acceptance of thoughts and emotions allows them to follow their natural functions without us getting caught up in them. When this occurs, healing and a sense of wholeness are brought about. The following are exercises for cultivating mindfulness.

Mindfulness Exercises

Mindful Breathing

The following exercise will allow you to develop the ability to slow down your thoughts and increase the power of your awareness.

1. Find a comfortable place to sit down. Try to find a place that offers solitude and is free of distractions. With practise, you will be able to do this in almost any environment, regardless of the distractions that may exist.
2. Close your eyes and allow yourself to relax. Breathing normally, place your attention on the flow of your breath through your nose. Focus on the sensations that you experience as you inhale and exhale. Notice the rising and falling

of your abdomen.

3. Continue to observe the flow of breath as it courses through your body. Feel yourself becoming more relaxed with each breath you take.
4. As you practise this technique, you are bound to experience your mind wandering as you get distracted by thoughts. As soon as you are aware that this has happened, gently redirect your focus back to the breath. Do not judge yourself when losing your concentration, regardless of how often this happens.

Note: getting distracted is the point of mindfulness. The secret is not to remain distracted. You get distracted, then notice that you were distracted and refocus your attention. Aim to get good at noticing when you are distracted, both when practising mindfulness and in other aspects of your life.

5. If you experience distracting sensations or emotions, do not judge these either. Simply accept these distractions without trying to change or avoid them and continue to focus on

your breath.

Mindfulness of the Sensations of the Body

Our bodies experience innumerable sensations, yet we are often unaware of them because we are so distracted in our daily lives. This mindfulness exercise will help you develop greater awareness of your body's sensations.

1. Lie down on the floor or a mat (using your bed for this exercise is discouraged as you may fall asleep.
2. Place your attention on the movement of your breath as you inhale and exhale.
3. As you follow your breath, become aware of the sensations of your body. Do you detect a tingling in your feet or hands? Do you sense pressure or stiffness in your back, shoulders, or neck? Allow yourself to experience every sensation that you are aware of. Do not try to change them, suppress them, or judge them as being good or bad. Simply allow yourself to experience them.
4. Notice that the sensations you feel are not stable. Some constantly change in their degree

of intensity, while others may seem to appear, disappear, and then reappear again.

5. Allow yourself to experience any given sensation for as long as you desire. When you are ready, move on to another sensation.
6. Be sure to continue breathing as you perform this exercise.
7. Continue to practise this exercise for as long as you wish.

Progressive Relaxation

Progressive relaxation is an exercise that relieves stress and promotes relaxation by sequentially tightening and relaxing the body's muscles. Besides relaxing the body and developing greater awareness of the body's sensations, doing this exercise before going to bed can be helpful if you have trouble sleeping.

1. Lie down in bed and allow yourself to relax and be comfortable.
2. Focus on your breathing for a few minutes, paying attention to your breath as it travels through your body during inhalation and

exhalation.

3. Close your eyes and breathe. Notice how your abdomen rises and falls as your breath flows in and out.
4. Feel the relaxation in your body as you breathe.
5. When you exhale, pay attention to the sensations in your body. Do you feel more relaxed?
6. Curl your toes. Hold it for a few seconds, and then relax. Feel the sensation of relaxation.
7. Tighten your thighs. Hold it for a few seconds, and then relax. Feel the sensation of relaxation. As you breathe out, feel your legs becoming heavier and more relaxed.
8. Tighten the buttocks muscles, hold them for a few seconds, and then relax. Feel the sensation of relaxation.
9. Tighten the muscles of your abdomen. Hold it for a few seconds, and then relax. Feel the sensation of relaxation.
10. Using your diagram, take three deep breaths. As you inhale, focus on your abdomen rising. When you exhale, focus on your abdomen

falling. After taking three deep breaths, inhale for a fourth breath and hold it. Hold your breath for as long as you can. When you exhale, focus on the sensations you experience.

11. Raise your shoulders toward your ears as high as possible. Hold for a few seconds, and then relax. Feel the sensation of relaxation.
12. Tilt your head back as far as possible. Hold it for a few seconds, and then relax. Feel the sensation of relaxation.
13. Raise your head toward your chest. Hold it for a few seconds, and then relax. Feel the sensation of relaxation.
14. Tighten your jaw. Hold it for a few seconds, and then relax. Feel the sensation of relaxation.
15. Raise your brow as high as possible. Hold it for a few seconds, and then relax. Feel the sensation of relaxation.
16. Tighten your brow as much as possible. Hold it for a few seconds, and then relax. Feel the sensation of relaxation.
17. Take time to relax and enjoy the sensations of your body.

Mindful Walking

Mindfulness can be practised anywhere and at any time, as it involves being aware of what is being experienced in the moment. The following is an exercise for walking in mindfulness.

1. When first practising this exercise, it helps to set a short distance (roughly ten meters for mindful walking. You can extend the distance as you become more comfortable with it.
2. With your route marked out, walk the distance at a relaxed pace. As you walk, focus on the sensation of the soles of your shoes as they make contact with the ground. Make sure that you continue to breathe as you walk.
3. As you become more skilful in focusing on the sensations of walking, you can extend your awareness of what is happening in your environment. Listen to the sound of birds singing, the wind blowing, the sound of cars, or the sound of people talking. As always, in mindful practise, do not judge, analyse, or evaluate anything you experience; your only job is to be aware.

Mindful Eating

Have you ever eaten while watching television or talking to someone, then realised that you have consumed your meal without any memory of doing so? Perhaps you realised that you ate your meal but had no memory of really tasting it? When we eat this way, we are not mindful of our eating. As a matter of fact, many problems with digestion or maintaining our proper weight are due, in part, to not eating mindfully. When we are not eating mindfully, we deny ourselves of savouring our food as our minds are elsewhere.

When practising mindful eating, it is important to set up your environment so that you will not be distracted as you eat. You can eat alone or find someone who would be interested in eating mindfully with you, meaning there is to be no conversation while eating.

Also, turn off all electronic devices and ensure you have everything you need to enjoy your meal, so you do not have to get up to get something while eating. Lastly, it is recommended that you eat a healthy meal. As the purpose of practising mindfulness is mental well-being, you also want to enjoy physical health.

1. Take time to relax and focus on your breath. Allow yourself to relax.
2. When you are ready, look at your food and observe its colour, shape, and texture.
3. Take in its aroma. How does your food smell? Is its aroma weak, mild, or strong?
4. Now, taste your food, but do so mindfully. Take only bite-size pieces and take your time before swallowing them. Allow yourself to savour its taste and notice how it feels in your mouth.
5. When you are ready, swallow your food.

Showering Mindfully

How many times have you taken a shower, only to realise that while your body was in the shower, your mind was somewhere else? You can practise mindfulness in everything you do, and showering is no different. Taking a shower mindfully is a great way to become more in touch with your body, its sensations, and awareness of the present moment.

When taking a shower, you want your full attention on the experience of taking a shower, not on your memories or your thoughts of the future. Your only job is to take in all the sensory experiences of taking a shower. It is only natural that thoughts will arise while taking a shower, which is okay. Do not react to your thoughts; notice, then let them pass and return your attention to the sensations of taking a shower. Allow yourself to experience whatever is happening at that moment.

As you take your shower, focus on what you are experiencing. Here are some examples:

- Pay attention to the feeling of the water running down your body.
- Feel the sensation of the water against your skin.
- Listen to the sound of your breath.
- Listen to the sound of the water cascading downward.
- Smell the shampoo or soap that you are using.
- Feel the sensations of the soles of your feet on the shower floor.
- Feel the sensations as you work the shampoo into your hair.

- Watch as the water glides down your body.
- Watch the water as it flows down the shower drain.
- Watch the water drop splatter as it makes contact with the shower floor.

Mindful Observing

Find a comfortable place—indoors or outdoors—to sit down and relax. For the next 10 minutes, be aware of everything around you and what you experience from within yourself (i.e., thoughts, emotions, sensations, or feelings).

Whatever it is that you notice, do not judge, evaluate, or analyse it. You are there to observe it. Feel free to go longer than if you can. Practise this each day, increasing the observation time each day. When doing this exercise, you should stay relaxed. You cannot get this exercise wrong. If you find judgements surfacing, let them go; allow yourself to experience this without judgment.

Practising mindfulness is also valuable when doing inner child work, another approach for transcending your self-sabotaging behaviour. The topic of the next chapter is inner child work.

Chapter Exercise

In your journal, write about what you experienced when you practised mindfulness. How did your experience practising mindfulness compare to when you were not being mindful?

Notes

Notes

We cannot be authentic as people until we learn to accept all aspects of ourselves.

Chapter 7
Inner Child Work

As children, all of us have experienced trauma in some form. The trauma I speak of can be as obvious as physical and sexual abuse or traumas that may not be as obvious, such as medical issues, accidents, poverty, or bullying. These traumas can remain with us into adulthood unless they are addressed.

The challenge is that many of these memories are subconscious, so we are unaware of them. Though we may not be aware of these memories, their energy affects us daily. Many of our stronger emotional responses result from these memories being triggered.

What is referred to as your "inner child" is these memories. Healing your inner child entails bringing resolution to these memories so they can be healed. To bring resolution to these memories requires that the light of your awareness will illuminate and heal them. As a result, you will be less likely to be triggered by them.

Doing inner child work offers incredible potential for personal growth. When your inner child remains in the subconscious, its reactivity will be reflected in your decisions and actions, such as self-sabotage. Your adult mind may rationalise your decisions and actions, but that does not address the root cause of the problem.

Inner child work involves revisiting these memories with your rational adult mind and bringing compassionate understanding to them. In doing so, your adult mind takes charge of them. When this occurs, your inner child will function to support your happiness.

This kind of healing will occur not only from within but also from without. Your inner child work will improve the quality of your relationships and other areas of your life. The reason for this is simple. Your inner child has tinted your view of yourself and the world around you. That view is tinted with fear.

When you do inner child work, this tinted lens is replaced by clarity and understanding. Your increased confidence and self-knowledge will show up in how you engage with the world around you.

Exploring the Inner Child

Janet is a young child whose parents are often critical of her and inconsistent in showing affection. In her attempts to please her parents, Janet starts to repress those aspects of herself that her parents are critical of and starts to adopt those that elicit affection. As Janet continues these efforts, the adopted aspects become more and more ingrained in her sense of identity while her repressed aspects are pushed deeper into her subconscious.

Though Janet's sense of identity has been moulded by her adopted aspects, her suppressed aspects retain their energies. These energies will continue to affect her emotionally and in her decision-making. For example, let's say that one of Janet's natural aspects is being easygoing. Her parents view this aspect critically because they believe that being easygoing will make their daughter an easy target for others to take advantage of. They also believe that she cannot be successful with an easygoing personality.

Janet picks up on the displeasure of her parents and starts to adopt the belief that she is not good enough and that something is wrong with her. Janet suppresses these beliefs and gradually adopts new ones, which she gets from modelling her parents. One of those beliefs is that being demanding of others and oneself is a sign of strength.

As Janet gets older, she will think and behave in ways that reflect this belief. It will become a part of her identity. However, she is still being influenced by her subconscious beliefs that she is not good enough. Because of this, she continues to doubt herself, and she develops a pattern of giving up on her goals, fearing that she will fail to achieve them. To return to her comfort zone, she engages in self-sabotaging behaviours as a way to save herself. She rationalises that she gave up on pursuing her goals because she was too busy or had more important things to do.

This Janet scenario represents how our unresolved, suppressed memories impact our life experiences. Additionally, these suppressed memories are authentic aspects of ourselves. We cannot be authentic as people until we learn to accept all aspects of ourselves.

The following are exercises for inner child work for you to journal on.

Exercise 1: What Do You Want to Change?

Directions: Select one or more of the following writing prompts to identify the patterns of thinking or behaving that you would like to change:

- I want to give up my resistance toward:
- I want to no longer feel triggered by:
- The part of me that I want to learn to accept and be at peace with is:

Exercise 2: Writing Prompts

Inner child writing prompts can be a powerful way to access your subconscious mind and connect with your inner child. Select the writing prompt or prompts that feel most relevant to you. When a writing prompt asks you to write from the child's viewpoint, try your best to step out of your adult mindset and try to perceive the situation through the child's eyes.

When you have accessed your childhood mindset, write down any memories you have of the events that occurred at that age. Also, write down any emotions you remember experiencing that were associated with those events.

When writing, do not think about it too much. Instead, write down whatever comes to mind. Let your writing flow as your thoughts appear. By doing this, you will gain insight into your inner child's pain. Select from the following writing prompts:

1. In your mind, visualise yourself as a child. As you visualise this, what do you notice? How does the child feel? What emotions come up when you imagine this?
2. If you could speak to your inner child at this moment, what would you tell them? What can you do to offer them support, love, or reassurance?

3. What could you do to reconnect with your body and support your inner child's physical well-being?
4. As a child, were there boundaries that you had difficulty with? How have those boundaries affected you as an adult?

Nurturing Your Inner Child

In the previous section, you explored your inner child by identifying patterns of thoughts and behaviours that do not support your happiness. Your inner child adopted these patterns to feel safe. The challenge is that we resist facing our inner child because the inner child is a source of painful memories. It is easier to rationalise or deny this pain's existence than face it.

Your inner child has been abandoned. You have disowned it by repressing its existence. The only way to feel like you are being your authentic self is to reconnect with your inner child and build trust. The following sections will guide you on how to start the process.

Creating a Safe Space

Before you can heal your inner child, you first need to gain its trust. From a psychological perspective, you need to be more compassionate with yourself. You can be more compassionate with yourself by being kind to yourself. Treat yourself the way you would someone who you deeply care about. By doing so, you will create less resistance toward yourself. By lowering your resistance to yourself, you will be able to understand the needs of your inner child better.

The following exercises are intended to generate greater self-compassion and to bring about relaxation or self-soothing. Learning how to do these things will allow you to regulate your emotions whenever you find yourself triggered by your subconscious memories.

Exercise 1: Validating Your Inner Child

Directions:

1. Think about those people you love and care about or those who make you feel safe. Make

a list of them.

2. Next, relax. You can do that by taking a couple of deep breaths. When you are feeling relaxed, imagine yourself as a child, being surrounded by the people you listed in Step 1.

As you imagine the people from your list, hear them telling you the following:

- "You make me so happy."
- "You're so special to me."
- "I want to take care of all your needs."
- "I will always be here for you."
- "I will keep you safe."
- "I am so proud of you."
- "You are so beautiful."

As you hear these words, pay attention to the feelings you are experiencing. Embrace those feelings and know that you are loved and accepted.

Exercise 2: Being Mindful of Breath

Being mindful of the breath is one of the oldest methods for calming the mind. It also demonstrates compassion for yourself and is a way to soothe yourself.

Directions: To do this exercise, do the following:

1. Get into a comfortable position.
2. Inhale deeply and exhale slowly. Repeat this step three times.
3. Breathe normally.
4. Close your eyes and focus on your breath. Notice the sensations in your body as you breathe in and out.
5. Whenever you find yourself getting distracted by your thoughts, notice them, thank them and release them. Then, return your attention to your breath.
    a. Remember, you are supposed to get distracted. Part of the practise is learning to notice distractions so that you can consciously decide whether to follow them.
6. Repeat this exercise daily until you feel comfortable and reach a calm state. Then, you can use it whenever you feel you need it.

Exercise 3: Write A Letter to Honor Yourself

Directions: In your journal, do the following:

1. Make a list of eight qualities that you most like about yourself. Examples of qualities may include:
    - Aspects of your physical appearance.
    - Aspects of your personality.
    - These are things that you have done in the past that you are proud of.
    - Any knowledge, skills, or talents that you may have.
2. Next, list how these qualities have benefited you in the past.
3. Finally, think about what you could do to honour those qualities.

Exercise 4: Create a Self-Care Plan

Directions: To create a self-care plan, do the following:

1. In your journal, make a list of the activities that give you a sense of well-being. When choosing your activities, include two types of

activities: impromptu and planned. Impromptu activities are ones that you can do anywhere at any time. Examples include:

- Doing breathing exercises
- Running
- Meditation
- Taking a walk.

Planned activities may require special equipment or a specific time or place. Examples include:

- Walking
- Swimming
- Going to dinner or the cinema.
- Spending time with friends
- Getting a massage

2. When you have completed your list, make two copies. Keep one copy at home. Put this copy where you will see it every day. This will serve as a reminder. Keep the second copy on your person so you will have it whenever you are out.
3. Commit each day to doing at least one of

your activities.

Healing Your Inner Child

Everyone has a wounded inner child, as no parent is perfect, no matter how much they loved and supported you. For example, a child may have had parents who worked most of the time to support them.

While the parents worked hard to give their child the best life possible, their absence may have created an emotional wound in the child, which became subconscious. The ability of adults to parent is only as great as their level of awareness. In turn, parents carry the wounded inner child they received from their parents. As adults, our wounded inner child may take on the form of our inner critic, that voice that tells us we are not good enough.

Healing your inner child involves acknowledging these memories and developing strategies that will allow you to safely get in touch with the wounded parts of your being. Doing this brings awareness to the wounded part of you without judgment. It is the same action a loving mother would take when trying to understand what her child is going through. Once one understands the nature of one's sufferings, one can develop healthy strategies to address them. To accomplish this, you first need to connect with your inner adult.

Your Inner Adult

The subconscious memories of your childhood continue to play out in your adult life and influence your thoughts and behaviours. In contrast, your inner adult is that part of you that can think rationally and make thoughtful decisions. It is the part of you that has always existed in you. However, in certain situations, it may become eclipsed by your subconscious memories, which absorb your attention.

Uncovering Emotional Wounds

You are not a single self but a conglomerate of separate selves, two of which are the inner child and your adult self. Healing comes when the adult self can communicate with the inner child, which is done through inner dialogue. Before the healing can occur, one must first understand the nature of the wound that needs healing. The following are exercises for conducting an inner dialogue with your inner child.

Exercise 1: Identifying Your Inner Child's Beliefs

1. Think back to a time as a child when you felt hurt or neglected. As you reflect on this, write down in your journal any words that come to you that describe how you felt about the experience:

Example:

- Abandoned
- Helpless
- Angry
- Scared
- Unloved
- Unworthy

2. Think about the statements your parents would frequently say to you and write them down.

Example:

- Why can't you listen?
- Why do you always do that?
- Stop being a baby!
- You drive me crazy!
- Stop your crying!

- Wait till your father comes home!

3. Next, reflect on your parents' relationship with each other.

Example:

- They frequently fought.
- They did not talk much with each other.
- My father was domineering and controlling.
- They did not spend much time together.
- There was tension between them.

The previous three steps of this exercise were intended to help you recall your childhood experiences. These experiences shaped how you felt about yourself as a child and may continue to affect your feelings about yourself as an adult.

4. Use your inner dialogue to connect with your inner child by becoming quiet and paying attention to whatever thoughts come to you. What negative beliefs did your inner child create about themselves based on the previous three steps of this exercise? You can use the following prompts to help you identify these beliefs:

- "I am _________."
- "I am not______."
- “I can’t__________.”
- "I will never_____."

The following are examples of beliefs:

- I am not a good person.
- I am not worthy.
- I can't trust anyone.
- I am not lovable.
- I will never be successful in life.
- It is my fault.
- I am stupid.
- I am ugly.

- I can't do anything right.
- I will never be successful.

5. Record your beliefs in your journal.
6. Reflect on what you experienced as a result of doing his exercise, and then answer the following questions:
   - What negative experiences from childhood continue to affect your life today as an adult?
   - How do these experiences impact your life today?
7. Reflect on these questions and write your response in a journal. When writing, include anything that comes to mind. By doing this exercise, you will have used your inner voice to connect with your inner child. You will have taken the first step in the healing process: identifying how your inner child impacts your life today.

Releasing Past Traumas

In the last section, you learned how to identify

the part of your inner child that needs healing. When you have identified it, the next step is to release past traumas from your mind and body. Painful memories from childhood, whether conscious or suppressed, create stress in the body. One approach to healing is to reduce that stress. Fortunately, one of the most powerful stress busters is your breath.

The challenge is that most of us do not breathe properly. We often take shallow breaths instead of deep breaths. Shallow breathing is often due to stress. It can start when we are young and become a habit that lasts a lifetime.

Mindful Breathing

Due to its simplicity, everyone can practise mindful breathing. Mindful breathing means paying attention to one's breath and the sensations that accompany it. When performing mindful breathing, you are deactivating the body's stress mechanisms and activating its relaxation response.

By bringing your attention to your breathing, you are brought into the present moment instead of being caught up in thought. Mindful breathing is often used in conjunction with different behavioural therapies, including dialectical behaviour, cognitive-behavioural, and acceptance and commitment therapies.

How Mindful Breathing Impacts the Mind and Body

Mindful breathing can bring about relaxation and improved moods, but how does it do this? The answer lies in the connection between our bodies and emotions.

How we use our bodies affects how we feel emotionally. For example, if you stand straight and hold up your head, you will feel more confident. You will feel less confident if you hold your head down and slump your shoulders. If you smile, you will feel happier than before you smiled. These are just a few examples of how changes in the body affect us emotionally.

If you are in a comfortable situation and feel relaxed, your breathing will slow and deepen. When stressed or anxious, our breath will be short and shallow. Often, we will breathe through our mouths and do not breathe fully. This restriction of airflow to the body may lead to feelings of tension, discomfort, and anxiety.

Mindful breathing techniques lower stress levels by making breathing intentional. They do this by getting us to notice the flow of the breath because we are breathing more deeply, the body's oxygenation increases, which triggers the body's relaxation response.

Benefits of Mindful Breathing

The benefits of mindful breathing are broad and encompass both the mental and physical realms.

Anxiety Reduction

Mindful breathing exercises activate the body's relaxation response, lowering heart rate and blood pressure and thus reducing anxiety. Because mindful breathing can induce a relaxed state, some believe it may also help reduce job burnout, anxiety, emotional exhaustion, and cynicism (Flook, 2013).

Reduced Negativity

Mindful breathing has been demonstrated to reduce negative thinking, which is often associated with individuals experiencing depression. The reduction of negative thinking is accompanied by improved mood (Zeidan, 2016).

Reduction in Depression

Research suggests that mindful breathing techniques can lower depression and PTSD symptoms. It is believed that these benefits are due to the activation of the parasympathetic nervous system (Zeidan, 2016).

Mindful Breathing

To perform mindful breathing, do the following:

1. Sit comfortably and close your eyes.
2. Breathe naturally as you focus on the sensations you experience as the air enters and leaves your body.
3. As you breathe in, say to yourself, "Breathing in, I experience calm." As you exhale, say, "Breathing out, I experience calm."

4. Fully experience the sensations as you breathe and focus on your breath's flow. Make the flow of your breath the focus of your attention. Let your breath flow naturally; do not attempt to control it in any way.
5. As you focus on your breath, feel the soothing experience that your breath brings.
6. If you have any concerns, surrender to them by returning your focus to your breath. Take refuge in the inner peace that your breath brings.
7. Maintain your focus on your in and out breath. Make this your anchor point whenever your mind wanders.
8. Whenever worrisome thoughts arise, allow them to appear, but return your attention to your breath. Do this deliberately and repeatedly until the thought fades away.

Another effective way to bring about emotional healing is through shadow work, which is the topic of the next chapter.

Chapter Exercise

In your journal, write about your experience doing the inner child exercises in this chapter. What did you learn from the exercises?

Notes

The shadow self refers to aspects of our personality that we have suppressed.

We have disowned these aspects of our personality because they were met with disapproval by ourselves or others.

Chapter 8
Shadow Work

In one of his plays, As You Like It, Shakespeare wrote, "All the world is a stage." Shakespeare meant that each of us plays a different role in life and that we all have our entrances and exits. We can expand upon this analogy by saying that we all have our own roles to play and that we also dress the part.

We wear masks to portray our characters and conceal those parts of ourselves that we are uncomfortable with. To our detriment, not only do we not reveal our faces to others, but we conceal our faces from ourselves!

The mask I speak of is the persona we want to promote to others. You know, it's about putting your best foot forward, even if it means lying to yourself! We do this because we are afraid of showing the world who we really are and of seeing the truth of who we are.

I knew a successful university professor who was well-loved by his students and his family. He had a great wit and a sense of humour, and he was very intelligent and well-spoken. Yet, he was very uncomfortable with dealing with others at the emotional level. He passed away without me ever really getting to know him as a person.

As I write this page, I find myself wondering what made him happy. Was he ever happy? What did he fear? What did he love? My friend wore his mask very well. I was very familiar with his character and role, but he remained a stranger to me when it came to knowing what lay hidden behind his mask. I am confident in one thing, though: I do not believe that he knew who he was beyond his role. The self-knowledge I speak of had been forced into the depths of his consciousness, lost within the abyss of his awareness.

In a way, consciousness is like the ocean. At a certain depth within the ocean, sunlight can no longer penetrate. This ocean layer is always dark. To a lesser or greater extent, we are all like my friend. We all suppress aspects of ourselves that we do not want to face. However, this suppression comes at a high cost, as we cannot be authentic with ourselves and others.

We are just as Shakespeare wrote; we play a role that meets the expectations of others.

What I have presented to you so far are different analogies for what is known as the shadow self. Each one of us has a shadow self. The shadow self refers to the subconscious aspects of ourselves, meaning that there are aspects of ourselves that we are unaware of. Though we are unaware of the shadow self, it impacts every part of our lives. As long as we suppress these aspects of ourselves, we will remain fragmented. We can only be made whole when we can integrate all aspects of who we are as individuals.

The purpose of shadow work is to bring awareness to the shadow self. Shadow work may sound a lot like inner child work, but there are important differences. Inner child work is about healing wounded aspects of ourselves, while shadow work is about bringing the suppressed aspects of us to the surface so they can be integrated.

If you dare to face your shadow self, you will be

richly rewarded. Exploring your shadow self leads to authenticity, personal awakening, and greater creativity. However, among the greatest rewards are a sense of inner peace and wisdom. This kind of growth will not only transform you but also lead to a more meaningful life.

The Shadow Self

The shadow self, often called "the shadow," refers to aspects of our personality that we have suppressed. We have disowned these aspects of our personality because they were met with disapproval by ourselves or others. By suppressing these aspects of ourselves, we lose all awareness of them.

The psychologist Carl Jung popularised the concept of the shadow self. According to Jung, we develop our shadow self during childhood. When we are first born, there is a wholeness to our personality, meaning nothing is suppressed. However, this wholeness is short-lived, as we will see in the next section.

How the Shadow Self is Formed

Long before they learn to use language, children recognise the meaning communicated through emotions. Emotions are an inherent part of being human and belong to our shared humanity. Additionally, part of our humanity is the need to feel secure and to belong.

Even the youngest child understands happiness, love, and kindness. However, they also recognise anger, sadness, and frustration. We quickly learn which traits and characteristics will be met with our caregiver's approval or disapproval. In other words, we learn to recognise when we are "being good" and "being bad." This kind of shaping of our personality continues as we get older and interact with more and more people. For example, on his first day of class, a first grader may behave aggressively and get scolded by the teacher for it.

At this early age, disapproval from figures of power threatens our need for security and belonging. In response, we learn to adjust our behaviours and adapt to the expectations of the world around us. One of our adjustments is to suppress certain aspects of ourselves. In other words, we begin the process of rejecting aspects of ourselves.

The aspects that get suppressed have little to do with whether they are positive or negative. Rather, they are suppressed if others see them as being unwelcome. Stated differently, any aspect of ourselves that is not consistent with how we want to be perceived is pushed into the deep recesses of our consciousness.

These suppressed aspects are what create our shadow self. We no longer accept them as being part of who we are. We no longer accept them, but we are also no longer aware of them! The following are examples of how the shadow self is formed:

Example 1

There is a sensitive young boy; he is in touch with his feelings. The boy is playing on the playground when he falls and starts to cry. His father responds by telling him, "Stop crying and be a man." The father, who has his own shadow self, believes that crying is a sign of weakness. Seeing that his father disapproves of his behaviour, the boy represses his sensitive side and tries to act tough.

When the boy grows up, he has difficulty expressing his feelings and showing emotion. This, in turn, causes problems in his relationships because he is afraid to show vulnerability.

Example 2

While shopping at the supermarket with her mum, a young girl becomes upset and throws tantrums. Her mother quickly responds by sternly telling her to stop being a bad girl. The girl starts to associate showing anger with being bad. She learns to suppress her anger. As an adult, she believes she must always come across as "having it all together." This causes problems for her because she does not know how to deal with her anger. As a result, she becomes passive-aggressive.

Example 3

A young girl is born with a strong sense of self. She knows what she wants and is not afraid to ask for it. Her parents keep telling her that she needs to stop being so demanding and that she needs to "tone it down." In this situation, the girl's confidence and strength are being rejected. To appease her parents, she rejects that aspect of herself. She grows up to be sweet, quiet, and obedient.

What is Shadow Work?

Shadow work involves bringing out our suppressed aspects from the depths of our subconscious and back into the light of awareness. Shadow work takes courage because it involves facing aspects of ourselves that we have spent most of our lives hiding from.

Shadow work involves facing truths about our lives with compassion for ourselves and the desire to live authentically. It takes compassion for us not to judge our shadow aspects. Facing our shadow aspects allows us to live authentically because shadow work restores our wholeness as human beings. We can live a life that is no longer fragmented by our disowning aspects of ourselves. In doing shadow work, you are healing and transforming your life.

Why Doing Shadow Work Is Important

The basis of everything in the universe is energy; everything that exists has energy as its fundamental component, including our thoughts and emotions. Even though we may suppress certain thoughts and emotions, their energies still exist. These energies will continue to build upon each other until they manifest as challenges to our emotional and physical well-being.

Even more profoundly, our shadow self plays a dominant role in influencing the conscious mind. What we often fail to realise is that many of the decisions that we make daily are not governed by conscious decision-making. Rather, our decisions are being dictated by our shadow self. In other words, we are running on autopilot!

Have you ever done something that you later regretted? Have you ever wondered how you could have done such a thing? The reason why you did that thing was that your shadow self was directing you. The impact of our shadow self on our lives can be vividly seen in our relationships.

Most relationship issues, intimate or professional, are created by our shadow self. Such issues are normally the result of projections. In other words, we project our shadow aspects onto others. An example would be a person who suppressed memories of a situation where they were taken advantage of when they were vulnerable. To distance themselves from these painful memories, they suppress that experience. When this person sees others acting vulnerable, they will view them critically.

The Benefits of Doing Shadow Work

Given everything, I have written so far, you may conclude that the shadow self is the realm of the dark side where negativity resides. However, this is far from the truth. Many positive aspects of us get suppressed. Further, recognising the darker elements transforms them in a manner that supports our emotional well-being.

1. Regaining Trust in Your Intuition

It is not uncommon, as children, that we are taught to distrust our intuition or gut. This may happen when children are reprimanded, without explanation, for unwanted behaviour. The adult is likely trying to keep them safe, but as the child, we only hear the reprimand and conclude that we are unable to trust our instincts when deciding what to do. We suppress this instinctual message and instead come to rely on doing what we have been told to do by others. When that happens, we may have trouble trusting ourselves. Our inner compass becomes the property of our shadow self. By doing shadow work, you can take back ownership of your intuition.

2. **Improve Your Decision-Making**

As noted, much of what we do is governed by our subconscious. Our shadow self is calling the shots, even when we believe we are making conscious decisions. This is because our shadow self is controlling our conscious decision-making. By bringing awareness to your shadow aspects, you render them powerless. The only reason our shadow selves have control over our lives is that we turn our attention away from them.

3. **Connecting with Your Strengths and Self-Empowerment**

Those with low self-esteem became that way because they have suppressed positive aspects of themselves. Because they are no longer aware of these aspects, they feel inferior. By doing shadow work, you can reclaim those positive aspects of yourself. In fact, doing shadow work can bring out strengths and abilities you may never know you had.

4. **Becoming Self-Actualised**

Life is about constant growth. If we are not growing, then we are declining. Our pursuit of personal growth is to become better and more effective people. Personal growth is about becoming more self-actualised, and one of the most powerful things you can do for personal growth is shadow work. As stated before, most of our behaviour is governed by the subconscious. Only by becoming aware of our shadow aspects can we move beyond the continued patterns of behaviour and thinking that stems from the shadow self.

How Do I Spot My Shadow Self?

Because we are so used to suppressing our shadow self, it is not always easy to spot. However, the exercises in this chapter will guide you in recognising it. In general, your shadow self-expresses itself in the following ways:

1. **Projections**

Our world (outer world) is a projection of our inner world. In other words, we project our shadow aspects onto others. In doing so, we believe that other people cause our upset. In truth, other people provide us with a mirror of what is going on within us. Example: I come across someone who I think is selfish and uncaring. If I look within, I will find that being selfish and uncaring are among my shadow aspects.

Note: To look within and check for shadow traits, I've asked myself, "What part of me is bothered by this?" or "What part of me notices this?"

2. **Triggers**

When we become triggered by someone or something, that person or thing reminds us of past trauma. Awareness of our triggers is important because they allow us to become conscious of the emotional wounds that need healing. In this chapter, you will learn to recognise your emotional triggers before reacting to them.

3. **Patterns**

We all have patterns of thinking, feeling, and behaving. Patterns are one way our shadow self tries to get our attention; our shadow selves want to be accepted and integrated with our conscious selves. Patterns are the repeated attempts of the shadow self-saying to us, "Notice me!" By doing shadow work, we can break the cycle of our negative patterns.

Communicating with the Shadow

One of Carl Jung's methods for learning about the shadow self was through what he referred to as "inner dialogue." Often used in psychotherapy, this method gives a person a means to communicate with the different aspects of their shadow self.

The following are various exercises for conducting inner dialogue. Before performing any of these exercises, I strongly recommend you get into a relaxed state and ground yourself.

The Mirror Technique (Am I mirroring?)

As discussed earlier, we project our shadow self on other people and situations to avoid facing these aspects of ourselves. It is also worth repeating that our shadows contain not only negative qualities but positive ones as well. An example is that you may find yourself drawn to someone due to their confident manner. The reason for your attraction is that you want to reclaim the confidence that has been repressed in you. Similarly, you may look down on someone who appears to be lazy when, in fact, you may be reacting to the same quality that exists within you.

The mirror technique is a useful exercise for recognising your projections. For this exercise to be effective, however, you will need to be brutally honest with yourself and willing to experience strong emotions. For this reason, the mirror technique may take practise practice before you experience results. The following are the steps for this technique:

1. As you go through your day, notice the thoughts and sensations that arise as you encounter others.
2. If someone elicits an emotional reaction in you, ask yourself, “Am I projecting something on them?” It should be noted that we sometimes project our qualities onto others with the same quality. For example, If I am angry, I may project my anger onto someone who is also angry. Psychologists refer to this as a projection of reality. For this reason, you want to ask, “Does this emotion belong to me, to them, or do we share it?”

When we are triggered, it is not always due to projection; however, it is in most cases. The mirror technique can be used to evaluate whether you are responding to your projections.

Conduct an Inner Dialogue

In this exercise, you will have a dialogue with the person or thing that created an emotional response in you.

1. To start, imagine the person or situation that elicited an emotional response from you. If you experienced an emotion but are unsure of what elicited it, give the emotion a form so that you can imagine it in your mind.
2. Next, express your feelings toward the imagined object. You can tell it things such as:

- You hurt me.
- I am so angry at you.
- You scare me.

You can also ask it questions to discover the reasons why it entered your life or why you felt that way. Examples of questions are:

- What do you want from me?
- What are you trying to tell me?
- What is going to become of me?

3. Next, listen to your inspiration or intuition as it answers your questions. What is it telling you? When you receive the answers, fully express the emotions that you are experiencing. Do not hold anything back. Whether the emotions are positive or negative, you will bring about healing by releasing them.
4. As you express your emotions, say out loud how you feel. Examples are:

- I am furious.
- I am hurt.
- I am heartbroken.
- I am in pain.

Honour your emotions by fully embracing them.

The 3-2-1 Method

The 3-2-1 method is all about integrating your shadow aspects with your whole self. Note: This exercise is best done in the morning when you first wake up:

1. When you wake up, take a moment to think about your goals and what you want to

accomplish.

2. Think of someone who elicited an emotional charge from you, be it positive or negative.
3. Hold the image of the person in your mind. Talk to the person or see yourself connecting with them.
4. In this step, you become the person by taking on their perspective of how they see things.
5. Before you go to sleep, select another individual who attracted or disturbed you during the day.
6. Hold the image of the person in your mind. Talk to the person or see yourself connecting with them. Become the person by taking on their perspective as to how they see things.

The 3-2-1 method can also be used with memories or dreams. Let's say I have a dream where someone is chasing me. The person or thing that is pursuing you is your shadow aspect, looking to be acknowledged. In the case of dreams, do the following:

1. Face the one that is pursuing you.

2. Ask them what it is they want you to know. Often, the pursuer will respond with a message like, “I am trying to keep you safe.”
3. Continue to face the pursuer until any fearful emotions dissipate.
4. When you feel like you understand the pursuer, see yourself incorporating the qualities of the pursuer into yourself. In doing so, you are integrating your shadow aspects.

Some people can do this exercise while dreaming. If you cannot do this, recall your dream when you wake up and then go through the steps.

Challenging Your Identity

Most of us think of ourselves as being good people. After all, we were conditioned to do so. As children, how often were we praised for being “good” boys or girls? At some level of our being, we develop a resistance to an aspect of ourselves that we do not perceive as being “good.” It is these aspects of ourselves that we sometimes repress as we do not want to acknowledge them. They do fit with the image of ourselves.

By suppressing any aspect of ourselves, we become fragmented. We fail to realise that nothing is intrinsically good or bad about anything in life. Concepts such as “good” and “bad” are solely the property of our minds. It is us who project “good” and “bad” onto our experiences.

When we can accept all aspects of ourselves, we can truly heal and return to a state of wholeness. This next exercise will start this journey:

1. In your journal, make a list of all your positive qualities.
2. For each item on your list, write an opposite quality for it. For example, if I list “generous” as being a positive quality of mine, I will write “selfish.” Without acknowledging this shadow aspect, it will impact my life by challenging the generous part of me. By acknowledging this aspect of me, I will learn that it is okay for me to be selfish at times.

Getting To Know Your Triggers

When someone pushes your buttons, you are triggered. Triggers are the people or situations that get us to react emotionally, often through anger. While most of us experience being triggered as a negative thing, this section will show you why being triggered is really a gift!

A simple way of thinking about triggers is that they are your shadow aspects that briefly make an appearance in the light of your awareness. The person or event that triggered you is not the source of your upset. Rather, they reflect your subconscious aspects that have yet to be healed. In other words, they remain as part of your shadow self.

When someone or something triggers you, it brings to light your subconscious beliefs about yourself. These beliefs are the fragmented aspects of yourself that seek to be acknowledged and accepted. When you get triggered, you are allowed to retrieve those aspects of yourself from the shadows and integrate them so that you can achieve wholeness. It is an invitation to look inward.

The following exercise can be used the next time you feel triggered. It helps you identify your shadow beliefs and heal them.

1. ***Breathe***

When you feel triggered, take a moment to breathe and get centred.

2. ***Identify the Feeling***

Let's say that someone says something to you that triggers you. Ask yourself, "How did I feel when they said that to me?" The feeling you identify will most likely be just a surface feeling, so you will go to the next step and dig deeper.

3. ***Going Underneath the Feeling***

Let's say that the feeling that is triggered is anger. The feeling of anger is a defensive mechanism that keeps us from experiencing our emotional pain. Because of this, you need to stop blaming other people or circumstances and take responsibility for your anger.

So, in this step of the process, you want to journey into anger. Treat the anger with compassion, just as you would if it was a friend suffering. Sit with the anger and take it in. Allow yourself to experience the feeling of anger fully. Be curious as to what arises from that feeling. It takes about a minute and a half to process a feeling. Pay attention to what you feel as you sit with your anger.

Identify Your Shadow Beliefs

As you spend time with the emotion, ask yourself what you believe caused you to be triggered. As with your emotions, the first belief you come up with will likely be a surface belief. For this reason, you want to dig deeper and uncover your shadow belief. Your shadow belief is contained in the thoughts and feelings that appear when you are triggered. The following exercise is for healing triggers, and it consists of two parts. For the first part, I will provide an example to show you how this exercise works.

Part 1

1. The first step is to ask yourself how you felt when you were triggered. My example will

be: “I felt unappreciated.”

2. My next step is to start a line of inquiry using the phrase "What would be so bad if...." So, my first question to myself would be, "What would be so bad if I was unappreciated?" After reflecting on this, I responded, "I would feel that I was unimportant.”
3. Now that I have an answer, I will drill down further by asking: "What would be so bad about not being important?" My answer to that question would be, "If I were not important, no one would care about me." I would then use my response and rephrase the question: "What would be so bad if no one cared about me? "My response to that question would be: "It would feel unloved." Consciously, I believe that I am being unappreciated. However, my subconscious belief is that I am unlovable. This is my shadow belief.

Part 2

Healing Your Triggers and Shadow Beliefs

Now that you have identified your shadow beliefs, you can start to heal them by working with them and integrating them into your whole self. Here is the process:

4. Take ownership of your shadow belief and recognise that it is just one part of you. Who you are is comprised of a myriad of different factors, and these factors include your beliefs. The shadow belief you identified is just one of those factors. You can think of it as a 2000-piece puzzle, and you have found one of those pieces. That one belief does not define who you are, just as one piece does not reveal the completed puzzle.
5. After you have claimed ownership of the shadow belief, have compassion for it. Your shadow belief is like a lost child and wants to be recognised. Further, this belief was formed when you were very young and has remained hidden for all that time. You were too young to discern the situation when your

shadow belief was created. If my shadow belief was, "I am unloved," that belief may have been formed when I was a small child, and my mother lost her temper because she was going through rough times. However, at that young age, I may have concluded that I was unlovable. By getting to know your shadow beliefs, you are showing compassion.

The following is an exercise for tuning into your shadow beliefs and offering them compassion:

1. Close your eyes and take a few deep breaths.
2. Breathe normally and get relaxed.
3. Ask yourself, "What part of me feels____________?" You would insert your shadow belief into the space. Example: "What part of me feels unlovable?"
4. Keep asking the question until you hear a voice or receive an image from that part of you.

Compassionately, listen to that part of you and connect to it.

5. Introduce your adult self to that part of you, and let it know that you oversee your life and that its services are no longer needed. Reassure that part of you that you will always be there if it needs you, that you love it, but that you are in charge.

Creative Expression

Art can be a powerful method for self-expression, which is why art therapy is frequently used to help people examine their inner worlds. For this reason, engaging in art is often used to learn about our shadow selves. To put this method into practise, do the following:

Put yourself into the desired state by recalling a situation that elicits negative emotions in you. Decide on what artistic medium you want to use, such as:

- Acrylic paint
- Watercolor
- Pastels
- Sculpture
- Pencil

Using your selected art medium, express the way that you are feeling. Do not worry about your level of creativity or what you should be creating, as none of those matters. Do not get caught up in your thinking; express how you feel. Let your hands guide you, and be spontaneous.

As you work to heal yourself, you want to set a direction for your life, which involves goal setting and motivation. The next chapter will discuss these topics.

Chapter Exercise

In your journal, write about your experience doing the shadow work exercises in this chapter. What did you learn from the exercises?

Notes

Notes

If you want to create a major change in your life, you need a clear understanding of what you want to achieve and a compelling reason for why you want it.

Ask yourself,
"What would achieving my goal give me?"

Chapter 9

Creating a Compelling Future

There is a story about a small army that sailed to a distant island where their enemy lived. The army's leader knew that his men would be outnumbered by their enemy. When the army disembarked on the island, the leader set the ship on fire. Bewildered by their leader's actions, the men asked the leader why he committed such an outrageous act. The leader told his men that he had taken away all their options and that their only choice was to defeat their more powerful enemy. They had no choice but to win.

If you want to create a major change in your life, you need a clear understanding of what you want to achieve and a compelling reason for why you want it. Having a clear vision of what you want to achieve will allow you to focus your attention in a way that is consistent with the goal that you are working toward. Having a compelling reason will keep you motivated despite the challenges that arise along the way. Knowing why you want to achieve your goals will drive you and keep you motivated.

To find your compelling reason, you need to first know what your "why" is. To find your "why", you'll need to continuously dig beneath the layers of your goal. The following is an example:

Let us assume that my goal is to increase my income. I would then ask myself, "What would achieving my goal give me?" Examples of responses to that question may be:

- I would better be able to provide for my family
- We would be able to enjoy a greater quality of life.
- I would feel more secure and have a greater sense of freedom.

Exercise: In your journal, write down one to three goals that you want to achieve.

For each goal, ask yourself, "What would achieving this goal give me?" Write out a list of your answers, and then pick the one that most resonates with you. This is your "why" for your goal.

How to Create Effective Goals

Now that you have found the "why" behind your goal, the next thing to do is to restructure your goal to increase its effectiveness. Two common reasons why many people do not achieve their goals are that they do not know their "why" and they do not structure their goals properly. Let's use my goal from the previous example: I want to increase my income. In its current structure, this goal is too general, making it unlikely that I will be able to achieve it. To be an effectively stated goal, it needs to be more specific. The goal needs to be measurable, indicate by what means, and have a timeline. Here is an example of how to make my goal more measurable:

Original goal: I will increase my income

My revised goal made measurable: I will increase my income by 20%.

Now that my goal is measurable, I need to indicate by what means I will accomplish it. The following is an example of this:

My revised goal, made measurable with indicated means, is: "I will increase my income by 20% by living on a budget and getting a second job.

My goal now is measurable, and it states how I will go about it. The final step is to add a timeline:

My revised goal was made measurable with means and timeline indicated: "I will increase my income by 20% within three months by living on a budget and getting a second job.

Written this way, I will know when I have reached my goal (I increased my income by 20%), how I am going to do it (getting on a budget and getting a second job), and how long I have to achieve it (three months).

The timeline component in goal writing is a target, not a deadline. If I do not increase my income by 20% within two months, it does not mean I failed. I can set a new target date if I do not meet the initial timeline. However, I should also reevaluate my goal and how I approached it to see if any additional adjustments are needed.

Keeping the Momentum

In the beginning, the pursuit of our goal's

achievement is often filled with passion and excitement. However, those feelings may dwindle as obstacles are encountered. Because of this, many give up on their goals out of frustration. It is for this reason that it is important that you keep generating momentum so that you can continue to push through, especially during the tough times. One way to keep the momentum going is to remind yourself of your "why," which we discussed earlier. I encourage you to do this daily. The following are other ways to keep your momentum going:

Act Now

When you set a goal, it is important that you act on it right away. It is easy to convince yourself that you will take action the next day, that you are too busy right now, or that you are too tired. Take some form of action immediately, regardless of how minor it may be. As an example, if my goal is to increase my income, I could hop online and start to familiarise myself with the different budgeting resources. Or I could think of the kind of part-time work that would work best for me. Regardless of what it may be, do something daily that will move you toward the achievement of your goal.

Team Up

When working toward your goals, having a team to support you and keep your momentum going is always beneficial. The following are suggestions for forming a team:

- Your "team" can be whatever you want it to be. The only thing that matters is that you can connect with someone willing to support you.
- When choosing a team member, find someone who you respect, who will hold you accountable, and with whom you can share your goals.

When you tell someone you respect that you will do something, you will more likely do it. If you can find someone who is also working on their own goals, you can support each other. To find such a person, start by thinking about what you are trying to achieve.

Let's say you are trying to become fit but do not

know someone trying to achieve the same thing. You could meet someone by asking yourself, "Where could I meet people who are trying to become fit?" A good place to start would be your local health club. Perhaps there is a recreational group that you can join.

Regardless of your goals, think about where you could meet like-minded people. Go there and find someone with whom you can connect.

Reward Yourself

When working toward achieving your goal, you are also changing your behaviour. If my goal is to run a mile each day, then that means my current behaviour is preventing me from doing so. For example, my current behaviour may be relaxing and watching television. So, when I am working on my goal, I am more focused on running and less focused on watching television.

When we work on goals, it is easy to fall back on our old behaviours. Even though I want to achieve my goal of running, there will be times when I do not feel like doing so. Perhaps I have unexpected responsibilities to take care of. Or I had a difficult day, and I am tired. Because of this, I may be tempted to go back to watching television instead of running.

Remember what was said earlier: all our behaviours are based on avoiding painful emotions or seeking positive ones. For this reason, it is important that you reward yourself anytime you move one step closer to achieving your goal, even if it is a small step.

Exercise: Make a list of things you enjoy doing. Include things that are free, low cost and extravagant. This is your reward list; it will serve you well, as we shall see.

Let's say I do not feel like running, but I get myself to put on my running shoes and run just to the end of my street. I made progress toward achieving my goal. For this reason, I need to reward myself for doing so. I'll choose something from my reward list and treat myself to it.

By rewarding myself each time I progress, my momentum will strengthen while my desire to return to my old behaviour will weaken.

The Day Before Your Death

Imagine this: you wake up in the morning knowing this will be your life's last day. How will you spend your last day on Earth? When people realise that their lives are ending, they often look back and regret what they have not accomplished. Perhaps they wish that they were kinder. Maybe they wish that they had spent more time with their family. Whatever regrets we may have in our final days, it is often too late to do anything about them.

Challenge: Every day for the next seven days: when you wake up, imagine it is your last day on Earth. You have 24 hours to accomplish everything you need to do to avoid deathbed regret. What is important to you now? To live this way, you will spend more time in the present moment, appreciate life, and live with greater meaning.

At the end of the week, reflect on your experiences in your journal. What reflections do you want to take forward with you into the rest of your life?

Break Down Your Steps to Success

We may lose momentum when pursuing our goals because our feelings about them may change. We may feel excited about pursuing our goals when we first set them. With time, however, we may become discouraged by the work we must do to accomplish them.

Before becoming a life coach and hypnotherapist, I had a rewarding yet personally unfulfilling career in educational leadership. I wanted to make a career change to inspire others to reach their dreams and guide them in unlocking their potential.

First, I embarked on a life-coach training and accreditation course. When I'd completed that, I added NLP and hypnotherapy modalities, all while still working full-time in educational leadership. Balancing the course, my three children and working full time was very difficult for me as my time for study was very limited.

I would listen to course recordings while commuting to and from work, when cooking and ironing, and even watch videos or course material while working out in the gym. Additionally, I would wake up early every morning to study.

I remember feeling overwhelmed. I struggled to keep up with my studies, and I was ready to drop out of the course. It was then that a thought came to me. I remembered a time when I was riding up a particularly steep hill on my bike. I felt that I did not have the energy to continue and reach the top. I decided to give up, ride back down and look for another, easier route. When I turned around to do so, I was surprised to see how far I had already travelled to get where I was. Having noticed my progress, I was freshly determined to get to the top, so I carried on. The memory of that experience helped me to see my current situation differently when I realised how far I had come in my course. It gave me the determination to stick with it.

I decided to focus exclusively on my course. Everything else in my life could wait, meaning no nights out with friends and family, no scrolling social media, and no mundane television. I broke down my coursework into small steps. I completed my practise, passed my assessments, and received my certification. I had reached the top of that steep hill! I made it through by focusing on one thing at a time.

It is important to keep up the momentum as you climb your own hills and mountains to personal success. Your climb will be made easier by breaking down your goals into steps and that will give you the momentum to keep going.

Let's say that your goal is to clean your house. Suppose you have been very busy for the last three months, so your house has not been tended to. As a result, a deep cleaning is needed. You feel like this will be a formidable task.

Instead of viewing it this way, break down this task into steps. You could approach this task this way:

1. Start by focusing only on the kitchen. Do whatever is needed to clean it, except mopping.
2. When you are finished with the kitchen, move on to the bathroom. Do whatever is needed to clean the bathroom, except mop.

3. When you finish cleaning the bathroom, focus on the living room. Do whatever is needed to clean it, except for vacuuming.
4. When you are finished with the living room, focus on the bedrooms. Except for vacuuming, do whatever is needed to clean them.
5. When you finish with the bedrooms, vacuum the house.
6. When you finish vacuuming the house, mop the kitchen and bathroom.

Focusing on one room at a time will make the task easier. With each room you finish, you will realise how much you have accomplished. Your momentum will keep you going until the house is clean.

Keeping Focus Long-Term

Several times in this book, I have mentioned how our minds are wired to avoid painful emotions and pursue pleasurable ones. This same dynamic causes us to focus on the short-term pleasures and disregard the long-term consequences. Similarly, this dynamic also causes us to avoid short-term pain, preventing us from experiencing long-term pleasure.

Here are some examples:

Focus on Short-Term Pleasure

- People who smoke will choose the short-term pleasure of smoking, ignoring the long-term potential for developing cancer.
- Children and young people may choose the short-term pleasure of playing video games, ignoring the long-term consequences of not keeping up with their schoolwork.
- A person may make purchases to experience short-term gratification, ignoring the impact those purchases could have on their finances in the long term.

Focus on Short-term Pain

- In the short-term, a person does not develop an exercise routine because of the effort it involves. However, they miss out on the long-term benefits of exercising.
- In the short term, a person may not save money. Because they feel that they deserve

to enjoy themselves, they spend their money instead. However, they miss out on the long-term benefits of financial security.

- In the short term, a person may not see a doctor regularly because they believe it is a waste of time. However, they may miss out on a healthier life when they get older.

Anything worthwhile in life takes deliberate effort and a willingness to endure short-term discomfort. For this reason, do not allow short-term pain to cause you to lose momentum. Instead, focus on all the benefits you will receive in the long term.

Chapter Exercise

In your journal, write about your experience doing the exercises in this chapter. Did any of the exercises change the way you feel about achieving your goals? If so, what changed for you?

Notes

Notes

The key to living a happy and fulfilling life has less to do with where we came from or where we are now.

Rather, it comes from a deeper understanding of ourselves.

Conclusion

In the rural area of India, a successful businessman was taking his morning walk when he encountered a beggar on the roadside. The businessman felt compassion for the beggar and invited him to have dinner with him that evening.

At dinner time, the businessman and the beggar enjoyed a grand feast and fine wines. Toward the end of dinner, the businessman noticed that the beggar had too much to drink and invited him to spend the night at his home. The beggar thanked the businessman and went to bed.

While the beggar was sleeping, the businessman sneaked into his room and took the beggar's robe. He then made a slit in the robe's lining and placed a precious jewel inside the robe. The businessman then returned the robe to the room. The next morning, the beggar thanked the businessman and went on his way.

Months later, the businessman was on his morning walk when he encountered the beggar again. Despite possessing a precious jewel, the beggar continued to live an impoverished existence.

What you have just read is based on the story, The Jewel and the Robe. The story is a metaphor for how we often are unaware of the wisdom that lies within us. The businessman symbolises the Buddha. The Buddha was not a god or a spiritual being. He was an ordinary man who became enlightened by looking within himself, gaining a deeper understanding of his true nature. The jewel in the story represents that deeper understanding. The beggar represents us when we are ignorant of our deeper nature.

The key to living a happy and fulfilling life has less to do with where we came from or where we are now. Rather, it comes from a deeper understanding of ourselves. It is through this kind of understanding that self-esteem, confidence, and nurturing relationships are forged. These are the things that lead to true success and a sense of greater purpose. I encourage you to be persistent in your efforts to discover the precious jewel that lies within you.

My final thoughts:

You come from love and it is to this nature that you will return; therefore, approach all activities in your life with love for both yourself and the world.

There is always the seed of good intention in everyone and in everything – actively look for it.

Your life is perfectly designed for your own growth and development – embrace the good and bad as opportunities for you to practise loving what is.

Thank you for your time and your energy in reading this book. It has been my pleasure to document and share my journey with you, and I hope it provides you with inspiration and guidance. I wish you all the very best with your transformation journey.

With loving regards, always

Nadine Ekiya Abeng

Stay in touch:

Share your thoughts on this book – please leave a review on Amazon (add link)

I'd love to hear from you and perhaps discuss any aspects of the book that resonated deeply with you.

Find and follow me on social media:

Facebook profile: **Nadine Ekiya Abeng**

Facebook Page: **Step into your power: Hypnotherapy with Nadine Ekiya Abeng**

Instagram: **@nadineekiyaabeng**

LinkedIn: **nadineekiyaabeng**

References

Flook, L. (2013). Mindfulness for teachers: A pilot study to assess effects on stress, burnout, and teaching efficacy. Mind Brain Educ. https://www.ncbi.nlm.nih.gov/pmc/articles/PMC3855679/

Goudreau, J. (2012). The Nine Ways Women Self-Sabotage. Forbes. https://www.forbes.com/sites/jennagoudreau/2012/02/08/the-nine-ways-women-self-sabotage/?sh=5dc9b34a320f

Lotus Pathway (2018). Stop Self-Sabotage by Rewiring Your Brain https://lotuspathway.com/blog/self-sabotage

Zeidan, F. (2016). Mindfulness meditation-based pain relief: a mechanistic account. N Y Academy of Science. https://pubmed.ncbi.nlm.nih.gov/27398643/

Made in the USA
Las Vegas, NV
02 April 2025